On Core
Mathematics

Middle School Grade 6

HOUGHTON MIFFLIN HARCOURT

Table of Contents Grade 6

COMMON CORE

Unit 6 Geometry

Unit 7 Statistics

Learning the Common Core State Standards

Has your state adopted the Common Core standards? If so, then you'll be learning both mathematical content standards and the mathematical practice standards that underlie them. The supplementary material found in *On Core Mathematics Grade 6* will help you succeed with both.

▶ Here are some of the special features you'll find in *On Core Mathematics Grade 6*.

INTERACTIVE LESSONS

You actively participate in every aspect of a lesson. You carry out an activity in an Explore and complete the solution of an Example. This interactivity promotes a deeper understanding of the mathematics.

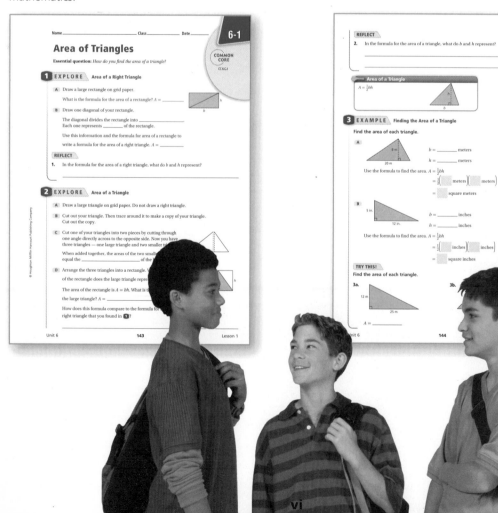

Getty Images/PhotoDisc

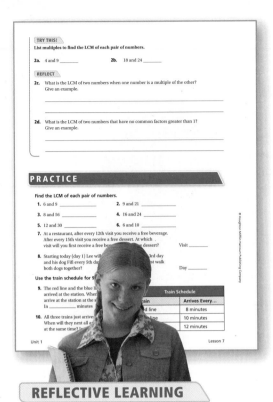

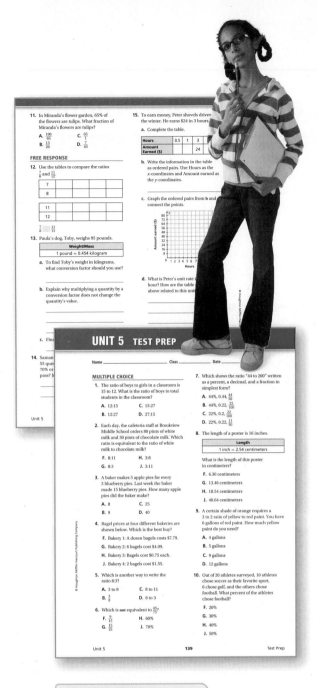

REFLECTIVE LEARNING

You learn to be a reflective thinker through the follow-up questions after each Explore and Example in a lesson. The Reflect questions challenge you to really think about the mathematics you have just encountered and to share your understanding with the class.

TEST PREP

At the end of a unit, you have an opportunity to practice the material in multiple choice and free response formats common on standardized tests.

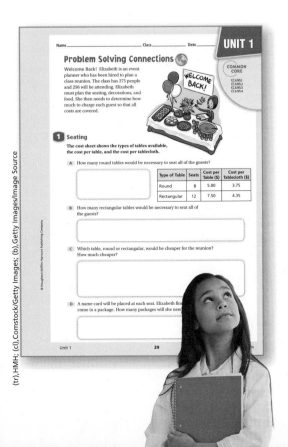

PROBLEM SOLVING CONNECTIONS

Special features that focus on problem solving occur near the ends of units. They help you pull together the mathematical concepts and skills taught in a unit and apply them to real-world situations.

Learning the Standards for Mathematical Practice

The Common Core State Standards include eight Standards for Mathematical Practice. Here's how *On Core Mathematics Grade 6* helps you learn those standards as you master the Standards for Mathematical Content.

① Make sense of problems and persevere in solving them.

In *On Core Mathematics Grade 6*, you will work through Explores and Examples that present a solution pathway for you to follow. You are asked questions along the way so that you gain an understanding of the solution process, and then you will apply what you've learned in the Try This and Practice for the lesson.

2 EXAMPLE   Using Exponents to Write Expressions

Use exponents to write each expression.

A $6 \times 6 \times 6 \times 6 \times 6 \times 6 \times 6$

What number is being multiplied? _____ This number is the base.

How many times does the base appear in the product? _____ This number is the exponent.

$6 \times 6 \times 6 \times 6 \times 6 \times 6 \times 6 = $ _____

B $\frac{2}{3} \times \frac{2}{3} \times \frac{2}{3}$

What number is being multiplied? _____ This number is the base.

How many times does the base appear in the product? _____ This number is the exponent.

$\frac{2}{3} \times \frac{2}{3} \times \frac{2}{3} = $ _____

② Reason abstractly and quantitatively.

When you solve a real-world problem in *On Core Mathematics Grade 6*, you will learn to represent the situation symbolically by translating the problem into a mathematical expression or equation. You will use these mathematical models to solve the problem and then state your answer in terms of the problem context. You will reflect on the solution process in order to check your answer for reasonableness and to draw conclusions.

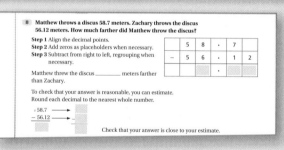

B Matthew throws a discus 58.7 meters. Zachary throws the discus 56.12 meters. How much farther did Matthew throw the discus?

Step 1 Align the decimal points.
Step 2 Add zeros as placeholders when necessary.
Step 3 Subtract from right to left, regrouping when necessary.

		5	8	.	7	
−		5	6	.	1	2
				.		

Matthew threw the discus _____ meters farther than Zachary.

To check that your answer is reasonable, you can estimate. Round each decimal to the nearest whole number.

  58.7 ⟶
− 56.12 ⟶

Check that your answer is close to your estimate.

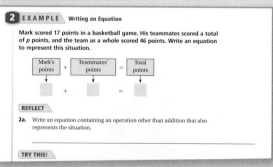

2 EXAMPLE   Writing an Equation

Mark scored 17 points in a basketball game. His teammates scored a total of *p* points, and the team as a whole scored 46 points. Write an equation to represent this situation.

| Mark's points | + | Teammates' points | = | Total points |

+   =

REFLECT

2a. Write an equation containing an operation other than addition that also represents the situation.

TRY THIS!

3 Construct viable arguments and critique the reasoning of others.

Throughout *On Core Mathematics Grade 6*, you will be asked to make conjectures, construct a mathematical argument, explain your reasoning, and justify your conclusions. Reflect questions offer opportunities for cooperative learning and class discussion. You will have additional opportunities to critique reasoning in Error Analysis problems.

3b. **Error Analysis** Marisol said, "Bailey's lemonade is stronger because it has more lemon juice. Bailey's lemonade has 3 cups of lemon juice, and Anna's lemonade has only 2 cups of lemon juice." Explain why Marisol is incorrect.

_____

_____

19. **Reasoning** The length of a particular object is x inches.

   a. Will this object's length in centimeters be greater than x or less than x? Explain.

   _____

   _____

   b. Will this object's length in meters be greater than x or less than x? Explain.

   _____

   _____

4 Model with mathematics.

On Core Mathematics Grade 6 presents problems in a variety of contexts such as science, business, and everyday life. You will use mathematical models such as expressions, equations, tables, and graphs to represent the information in the problem and to solve the problem. Then you will interpret your results in the problem context.

Essential question: *How can you use equations, tables, and graphs to represent relationships between two variables?*

COMMON CORE

CC.6.EE.9

1 EXPLORE Equations in Two Variables

Tina is buying DVDs from an online store. Each DVD costs $8, and there is a flat fee of $6 for shipping.

Let x represent the number of DVDs that Tina buys. Let y represent Tina's total cost. An equation in two variables can represent the relationship between x and y.

Total cost	=	Cost per DVD	·	Number of DVDs	+	Cost of shipping
y	=	8	·	x	+	6

Complete the table.

DVDs Bought x	$8x + 6$	Total Cost y ($)
1	8(1) + 6	14
2	8( ) + 6	
3	8( ) + 6	
4	8( ) + 6	
5	8( ) + 6	
6	8( ) + 6	
7	8( ) + 6	

REFLECT

1a. Look at the y-values in the right column of the table. What pattern do you see? What does this pattern mean in the problem?

_____

_____

1b. A **solution of an equation in two variables** is an ordered pair (x, y) that makes the equation true. The ordered pair (1, 14) is a solution of $y = 8x + 6$. Write the other solutions from the table as ordered pairs.

_____

⑤ Use appropriate tools strategically.

You will use a variety of tools in *On Core Mathematics Grade 6*, including manipulatives, paper and pencil, and technology. You might use manipulatives to develop concepts, paper and pencil to practice skills, and technology (such as graphing calculators, spreadsheets, or geometry software) to investigate more complicated mathematical ideas.

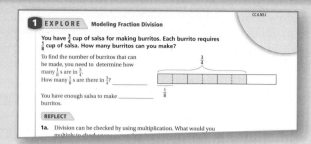

CC.6.NS.1

1 EXPLORE Modeling Fraction Division

You have $\frac{3}{4}$ cup of salsa for making burritos. Each burrito requires $\frac{1}{8}$ cup of salsa. How many burritos can you make?

To find the number of burritos that can be made, you need to determine how many $\frac{1}{8}$ s are in $\frac{3}{4}$.

How many $\frac{1}{8}$ s are there in $\frac{3}{4}$? _____

You have enough salsa to make _____ burritos.

REFLECT

1a. Division can be checked by using multiplication. What would you multiply to check

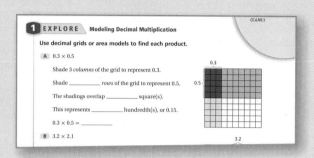

CC.6.NS.3

1 EXPLORE Modeling Decimal Multiplication

Use decimal grids or area models to find each product.

A 0.3×0.5

Shade 3 *columns* of the grid to represent 0.3.

Shade _____ *rows* of the grid to represent 0.5.

The shadings overlap _____ square(s).

This represents _____ hundredth(s), or 0.15.

$0.3 \times 0.5 =$ _____

B 3.2×2.1

⑥ Attend to precision.

Precision refers not only to the correctness of arithmetic calculations, algebraic manipulations, and geometric reasoning but also to the proper use of mathematical language, symbols, and units to communicate mathematical ideas. Throughout *On Core Mathematics Grade 6* you will demonstrate your skills in these areas when you are asked to calculate, describe, show, explain, prove, and predict.

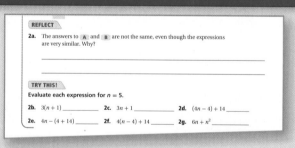

REFLECT

2a. The answers to **A** and **B** are not the same, even though the expressions are very similar. Why?

_____

_____

TRY THIS!

Evaluate each expression for $n = 5$.

2b. $3(n + 1)$ _____   **2c.** $3n + 1$ _____   **2d.** $(4n - 4) + 14$ _____

2e. $4n - (4 + 14)$ _____   **2f.** $4(n - 4) + 14$ _____   **2g.** $6n + n^2$ _____

REFLECT

1a. Lisa evaluated the expressions $2x$ and x^2 for $x = 2$ and found that both expressions were equal to 4. Lisa concluded that $2x$ and x^2 are equivalent expressions. How could you show Lisa that she is incorrect?

_____

_____

1b. What does **1a** demonstrate about expressions?

_____

_____

In *On Core Mathematics Grade 6*, you will look for patterns or regularity in mathematical structures such as expressions, equations, operations, geometric figures, and diagrams. You will use these patterns to generalize beyond a specific case and to make connections between related problems.

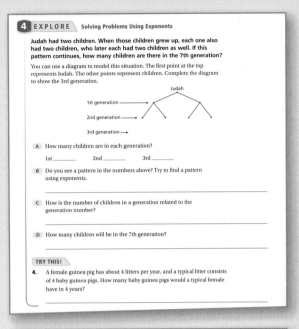

4 EXPLORE   Solving Problems Using Exponents

Judah had two children. When those children grew up, each one also had two children, who later each had two children as well. If this pattern continues, how many children are there in the 7th generation?

You can use a diagram to model this situation. The first point at the top represents Judah. The other points represent children. Complete the diagram to show the 3rd generation.

A How many children are in each generation?

1st _____   2nd _____   3rd _____

B Do you see a pattern in the numbers above? Try to find a pattern using exponents.

_____

C How is the number of children in a generation related to the generation number?

_____

D How many children will be in the 7th generation?

_____

TRY THIS!

4. A female guinea pig has about 4 litters per year, and a typical litter consists of 4 baby guinea pigs. How many baby guinea pigs would a typical female have in 4 years?

_____

CC.6.EE.6

1 EXPLORE   Using Variables to Describe Patterns

Look at the pattern of squares below.

Stage 1   Stage 2   Stage 3

A What is the pattern? _____

How many squares will be in stage 4? _____

B What is the relationship between the stage number and the number of squares?

_____

Use this relationship to complete the table below.

Stage	1	2	3	4	5	6	7	8	
Squares	3	6	9						

C Let *n* represent any stage number. How many squares are in stage *n*?

_____

Add a column to the end of the table in **B** for stage *n*.

REFLECT

1. When might it be useful to know how many squares are in stage *n*?

UNIT 1
```

# The Number System: Fractions and Decimals

## Unit Focus

You have already learned how to multiply and divide whole numbers. In this unit, you will learn how to divide multi-digit numbers and fractions. You will also learn how to add, subtract, multiply, and divide decimals. You will then learn how to find the greatest common factor and least common multiple of two numbers.

## Unit at a Glance

COMMON CORE

| Lesson | | Standards for Mathematical Content |
|---|---|---|
| 1-1 | Dividing Multi-Digit Numbers | CC.6.NS.2 |
| 1-2 | Dividing Fractions | CC.6.NS.1 |
| 1-3 | Adding and Subtracting Decimals | CC.6.NS.3 |
| 1-4 | Multiplying Decimals | CC.6.NS.3 |
| 1-5 | Dividing Decimals | CC.6.NS.3 |
| 1-6 | Greatest Common Factor | CC.6.NS.4 |
| 1-7 | Least Common Multiple | CC.6.NS.4 |
| | Problem Solving Connections | |
| | Test Prep | |

UNIT 1
```

Unpacking the Common Core State Standards

Use the table to help you understand the Standards for Mathematical Content that are taught in this unit. Refer to the lessons listed after each standard for exploration and practice.

COMMON CORE Standards for Mathematical Content	What It Means For You
CC.6.NS.1 Interpret and compute quotients of fractions, and solve word problems involving division of fractions by fractions, e.g., by using visual fraction models and equations to represent the problem. Lesson 1-2	You will learn how to divide two fractions, and you will understand the relationship between multiplication and division.
CC.6.NS.2 Fluently divide multi-digit numbers using the standard algorithm. Lesson 1-1	You will learn how to divide multi-digit numbers by using long division.
CC.6.NS.3 Fluently add, subtract, multiply, and divide multi-digit decimals using the standard algorithm for each operation. Lessons 1-3, 1-4, 1-5	You will use your knowledge of adding, subtracting, multiplying, and dividing whole numbers to perform the same operations with decimals.
CC.6.NS.4 Find the **greatest common factor of two whole numbers less than or equal to 100** and the least common multiple of two whole numbers less than or equal to 12. Use the distributive property to express a sum of two whole numbers 1–100 with a common factor as a multiple of a sum of two whole numbers with no common factor. Lesson 1-6	You will determine factors of numbers and the greatest common factor of two numbers. You will use the greatest common factor to decide how to share or distribute items in a collection.
CC.6.NS.4 Find the greatest common factor of two whole numbers less than or equal to 100 and the **least common multiple of two whole numbers less than or equal to 12.** Use the distributive property to express a sum of two whole numbers 1–100 with a common factor as a multiple of a sum of two whole numbers with no common factor. Lesson 1-7	You will determine the least common multiple of two numbers and solve real-world problems involving the least common multiple.

Dividing Multi-Digit Numbers

1-1

COMMON CORE

CC.6.NS.2

Essential question: *How do you divide multi-digit numbers?*

1 EXPLORE **Estimating Quotients**

A local petting zoo had a total of 98,464 visitors last year. The zoo was open every day except Thanksgiving, Christmas, and New Year's Day. Estimate the average number of visitors per day.

A To find the average number of visitors per day, you need to divide. To estimate the quotient, first estimate the dividend by rounding the number of visitors to the nearest ten thousand.

$$\overset{\text{quotient}}{\text{divisor}\overline{)\text{dividend}}}$$

98,464 rounded to the nearest ten thousand is _____.

B There were 365 days last year. How many days was the petting

zoo open? _____

C Estimate the divisor by rounding the number of days that the zoo was open to the nearest hundred.

_____ rounded to the nearest hundred is _____.

D Estimate the quotient. _____ ÷ _____ = _____

The average number of visitors per day last year was about _____.

REFLECT

1a. How can you check that your quotient is correct?

_____

_____

1b. Do you think that your estimate is greater than or less than the actual answer? Explain.

_____

_____

1c. **Error Analysis** A student said there were 250 visitors at the zoo each day last year. Explain why this is incorrect.

_____

_____

The exact average number of visitors per day is the quotient of 98,464 and 362. This quotient can be found by using long division.

2 EXAMPLE Long Division

A local petting zoo had a total of 98,464 visitors last year. The zoo was open every day except Thanksgiving, Christmas, and New Year's Day. What was the average number of visitors per day?

Step 1 362 is greater than 9 and 98, so divide 984 by 362. Place the first digit in the quotient in the hundreds place. Multiply 2 by 362 and place the product under 984. Subtract.

$$
\begin{array}{r}
2 \\
362\overline{)98{,}464} \\
-72\ 4 \\
\hline
26\ 0
\end{array}
$$

Step 2 Bring down the tens digit. Divide 2,606 by 362. Multiply 7 by 362 and place the product under 2,606. Subtract.

$$
\begin{array}{r}
27 \\
362\overline{)98{,}464} \\
-72\ 4\!\!\downarrow \\
\hline
26\ 06 \\
-25\ 34 \\
\hline
72
\end{array}
$$

Step 3 Bring down the ones digit. Divide the ones.

$$
\begin{array}{r}
27\ \square \\
362\overline{)98{,}464} \\
-72\ 4 \\
\hline
26\ 06 \\
-25\ 34\!\!\downarrow \\
\hline
72\ \square \\
- \\
\hline
\square
\end{array}
$$

The average number of visitors per day last year was _____.

REFLECT

2a. How does your estimate in ❶ compare to the actual average number of visitors per day? How does this compare to your prediction from **1b**?

_____

_____

2b. How can you check that your quotient is correct?

_____

_____

2c. **What if…?** If the zoo had been open fewer days but the attendance for the year was the same, would the average number of visitors per day be greater than or less than the quotient you calculated?

_____

3 EXAMPLE   Long Division with a Remainder

Callie has 1,850 books. She must pack them into boxes to ship to a bookstore. Each box holds 12 books. How many boxes will she need to pack all of the books?

Divide 1,850 by 12.

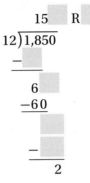

$$
\begin{array}{r}
15\ \ \ R\ \ \\
12\overline{)1{,}850}\\
-\ \ \ \ \\
\hline
6\ \ \ \\
-60\ \ \\
\hline
\\
-\ \ \\
\hline
2\\
\end{array}
$$

Notice that the numbers do not divide evenly. There is a remainder. What does the remainder mean in this situation?

_____

_____

How many boxes does Callie need to pack the books? _____ boxes
Explain.

_____

_____

TRY THIS!

3a. Divide 5,796 by 28. _____

3b. $67\overline{)3{,}098}$

PRACTICE

Divide.

1. 2,226 ÷ 53 _____

2. Divide 4,514 by 74. _____

3. $83\overline{)2{,}001}$

4. 3,493 ÷ 37 _____

5. Divide 18,156 by 267. _____

6. $438\overline{)35{,}506}$

7. 23,712 ÷ 247 _____

8. $313\overline{)39{,}760}$

Divide.

9. $1,643 \div 53$ _____

10. Divide 578 by 34. _____

11. $134\overline{)3,685}$

12. $423 \div 12$ _____

13. Divide 819 by 117. _____

14. $92\overline{)598}$

15. $10,626 \div 21$ _____

16. $24\overline{)6,339}$

17. A theater has 1,120 seats in 35 equal rows. How many seats are in each row?

_____ seats

18. At a wedding reception, there will be 1,012 guests. A round table will seat 12 guests. How many tables will be needed?

_____ tables

19. Emilio has 8,450 trees to plant in rows on his tree farm. He will plant 115 trees per row. How many rows of trees will he have?

_____ rows

20. Camila has 1,296 beads to make bracelets. Each bracelet will contain 24 beads. How many bracelets can she make?

_____ bracelets

21. The table shows the number of miles that Awan drove over six months. Find the average number of miles per day for each month.

January: _____ miles

February: _____ miles

March: _____ miles

April: _____ miles

May: _____ miles

June: _____ miles

Month	Number of Days	Miles Traveled
January	31	1,922
February	28	2,940
March	31	3,565
April	30	3,630
May	31	2,418
June	30	3,510

22. **Reasoning** How is the quotient $80,000 \div 2,000$ different from the quotient $80,000 \div 200$ or $80,000 \div 20$?

_____

_____

23. **Reasoning** Given that $9,554 \div 562 = 17$, how can you find the quotient $95,540 \div 562$?

_____

_____

Dimding Fractions

Essential question: *How do you divide fractions?*

1 EXPLORE Modeling Fraction Division

You have $\frac{3}{4}$ cup of salsa for making burritos. Each burrito requires $\frac{1}{8}$ cup of salsa. How many burritos can you make?

To find the number of burritos that can
be made, you need to determine how
many $\frac{1}{8}$ s are in $\frac{3}{4}$.
How many $\frac{1}{8}$ s are there in $\frac{3}{4}$? _____

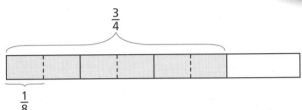

You have enough salsa to make _____
burritos.

REFLECT

1a. Division can be checked by using multiplication. What would you
multiply to check your answer above?

_____

TRY THIS!

1b. How many burritos could you make with $\frac{1}{2}$ cup of salsa? _____

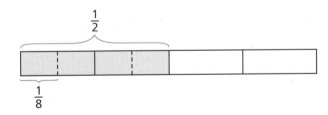

1c. Five people share $\frac{1}{2}$ pound of chocolate equally. How much chocolate

does each person receive? _____ pound

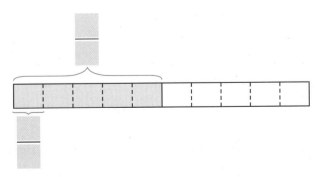

Another way to divide fractions is to use *reciprocals.*
Two numbers whose product is 1 are **reciprocals**. To find the
reciprocal of a fraction, switch the numerator and denominator.

$$\frac{\text{numerator}}{\text{denominator}} \cdot \frac{\text{denominator}}{\text{numerator}} = 1$$

2 EXAMPLE   Reciprocals

Find the reciprocal of each fraction or mixed number.

A $\frac{5}{8}$

Switch the numerator and denominator: ——

The reciprocal of $\frac{5}{8}$ is ——.

Check:

$$\frac{}{} \times \frac{5}{8} = \frac{}{} = 1$$

B $\frac{1}{6}$

Switch the numerator and denominator: ——

Simplify: ▢

The reciprocal of $\frac{1}{6}$ is ▢.

C $1\frac{2}{7}$

Change to an improper fraction: $1\frac{2}{7} = \dfrac{}{}$

Switch the numerator and denominator: ——

The reciprocal of $1\frac{2}{7}$ is ——.

TRY THIS!

Find the reciprocal of each fraction or mixed number.

2a. $\frac{7}{8}$ _____

2b. $\frac{9}{15}$ _____

2c. $\frac{1}{11}$ _____

2d. $2\frac{4}{5}$ _____

REFLECT

2e. Is any number its own reciprocal? If so, what number(s)?

_____

2f. Does every number have a reciprocal? Explain.

_____

2g. The reciprocal of a whole number is a fraction with _____ in the numerator.

Notice that dividing by a whole number is equivalent to multiplying by its reciprocal. This is also true when dividing by fractions. To divide by a fraction, multiply by its reciprocal.

$$24 \div 3 = 8$$
$$24 \times \frac{1}{3} = 8$$

3 EXAMPLE   Using Reciprocals to Divide Fractions

Divide.

A $\frac{5}{8} \div \frac{5}{6}$

Step 1 Rewrite the problem as multiplication using the reciprocal of the second fraction.

$$\frac{5}{8} \div \frac{5}{6} = \frac{5}{8} \times \underline{}$$

Step 2 Multiply and simplify.

$$\frac{5}{8} \times \underline{} = \frac{30}{40}$$

$$\frac{30}{40} = \underline{}$$

$$\frac{5}{8} \div \frac{5}{6} = \underline{}$$

B $1\frac{3}{7} \div \frac{2}{5}$

Step 1 Convert the mixed number to a fraction.

$$1\frac{3}{7} = \underline{}$$

Step 2 Rewrite the problem as multiplication using the improper fraction and the reciprocal of the second fraction.

$$1\frac{3}{7} \div \frac{2}{5} = \underline{} \div \frac{2}{5} = \underline{} \times \underline{}$$

Step 3 Multiply and simplify.

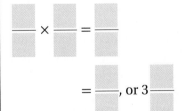

$$\underline{} \times \underline{} = \underline{}$$

$$= \underline{}, \text{ or } 3\underline{}$$

$$1\frac{3}{7} \div \frac{2}{5} = \underline{}$$

TRY THIS!

Divide.

3a. $\frac{9}{10} \div \frac{2}{5} = \underline{}$

3b. $2\frac{9}{10} \div \frac{3}{5} = \underline{}$

4 EXAMPLE Solving Problems Involving Area

The area of a rectangular flower bed is $6\frac{1}{2}$ square feet. The width of the flower bed is $\frac{3}{4}$ feet. What is the length? (*Hint:* area = length × width)

To find the length of the flower bed, divide the area by the width.

$6\frac{1}{2} \div \frac{3}{4} = \dfrac{}{} \div \frac{3}{4}$

$= \dfrac{}{} \times \dfrac{}{} = \dfrac{}{} = \dfrac{}{} = \dfrac{}{}$

$A = 6\frac{1}{2}$ ft²	$w = \frac{3}{4}$ ft
$\ell = ?$	

The length of the flower bed is _____ feet.

PRACTICE

Find the reciprocal of each fraction or mixed number.

1. $\frac{2}{5}$ _____

2. $\frac{1}{9}$ _____

3. $\frac{5}{3}$ _____

4. $\frac{4}{11}$ _____

5. $4\frac{1}{5}$ _____

6. $3\frac{1}{8}$ _____

Divide.

7. $\frac{4}{3} \div \frac{5}{3} =$ _____

8. $\frac{3}{10} \div \frac{4}{5} =$ _____

9. $\frac{1}{2} \div \frac{2}{5} =$ _____

10. $\frac{8}{9} \div \frac{1}{2} =$ _____

11. $4\frac{1}{4} \div \frac{3}{4} =$ _____

12. $4 \div 1\frac{1}{8} =$ _____

13. A recipe for one loaf of banana bread requires $\frac{2}{3}$ cup of oil. You have 2 cups of oil. How many loaves of banana bread can you make? _____ loaves

14. Ayita made $5\frac{1}{2}$ cups of trail mix. She wants to divide the trail mix into $\frac{3}{4}$ cup servings. How many servings will she have? _____ serving(s)

15. Dao has $2\frac{3}{8}$ pounds of hamburger meat. He is making $\frac{1}{4}$-pound burgers. How many hamburgers can he make? _____ hamburger(s)

16. A rectangular piece of land has an area of $\frac{3}{4}$ square mile and is $\frac{1}{2}$ mile wide. What is the length? _____ mile(s)

17. Write a real-world problem whose solution requires dividing the fractions $\frac{1}{3}$ and $\frac{3}{4}$. Then solve your problem.

_____

_____

Adding and Subtracting Decimals

Essential question: *How do you add and subtract decimals?*

1 EXPLORE   Modeling Decimal Addition

A chemist combines 0.17 mL of water and 0.49 mL of hydrogen peroxide in a beaker. How much total liquid is in the beaker?

You can use a decimal grid divided into 100 small squares to solve this problem. The entire decimal grid represents 1 unit, so each small square represents 0.01, or 1 one-hundredth.

Water	**+**	**Hydrogen Peroxide**	**=**	**Total**

How many squares are shaded to represent 0.17 mL of water?

_____

How many squares are shaded to represent 0.49 mL of hydrogen peroxide? _____

How many total squares are shaded?

_____

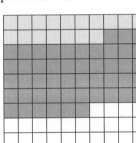

$0.17 + 0.49 =$ _____

There are _____ mL of liquid in the beaker.

TRY THIS!

Shade the grid to find each sum.

1a. $0.24 + 0.71 =$ _____

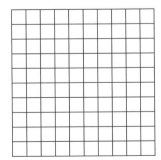

1b. $0.08 + 0.65 =$ _____

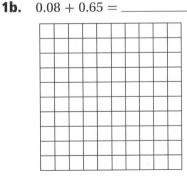

Adding and subtracting decimals are very similar to adding and subtracting whole numbers. First align the numbers by place value. Start adding or subtracting at the right and regroup when necessary. Bring down the decimal point into your answer.

2 EXAMPLE **Adding Decimals**

Hector rode his bicycle 3.12 miles on Monday and 4.7 miles on Tuesday. How many miles did he ride in all?

Step 1 Align the decimal points.
Step 2 Add zeros as placeholders when necessary.
Step 3 Add from right to left.

	3	.	1	2
+	4	.	7	0
		.		

Hector rode _____ miles in all.

To check that your answer is reasonable, you can estimate.
Round each decimal to the nearest whole number.

$$
\begin{array}{r}
3.12 \\
+ 4.70 \\
\hline
7.82
\end{array}
\longrightarrow
\begin{array}{r}
3 \\
+ 5 \\
\hline
8
\end{array}
$$

Since 8 is close to 7.82, the answer is reasonable.

TRY THIS!

Add.

2a. $0.42 + 0.27 =$ _____

2b. $0.61 + 0.329 =$ _____

2c. $3.25 + 4.6 =$ _____

2d. $17.27 + 3.88 =$ _____

REFLECT

2e. Why can you rewrite 4.7 as 4.70?

_____

_____

2f. Why is it important to align the decimal points when adding?

_____

_____

3 EXAMPLE   Subtracting Decimals

A   Mia is 160.2 centimeters tall. Rosa is 165.1 centimeters tall.
How much taller is Rosa than Mia?

Step 1 Align the decimal points.
Step 2 Add zeros as placeholders when necessary.
Step 3 Subtract from right to left, regrouping when
necessary.

		1	6	5	.	1
−		1	6	0	.	2
					.	

Rosa is _____ centimeters taller than Mia.

To check that your answer is reasonable, you can estimate.
Round each decimal to the nearest whole number.

165.1 ⟶ ☐
− 160.2 ⟶ − ☐
☐   ☐   Check that your answer is close to your estimate.

B   Matthew throws a discus 58.7 meters. Zachary throws the discus
56.12 meters. How much farther did Matthew throw the discus?

Step 1 Align the decimal points.
Step 2 Add zeros as placeholders when necessary.
Step 3 Subtract from right to left, regrouping when
necessary.

		5	8	.	7	0
−		5	6	.	1	2
				.		

Matthew threw the discus _____ meters farther
than Zachary.

To check that your answer is reasonable, you can estimate.
Round each decimal to the nearest whole number.

58.7 ⟶ ☐
− 56.12 ⟶ − ☐
☐   ☐   Check that your answer is close to your estimate.

TRY THIS!

Subtract.

3a. $0.91 − 0.45 =$ _____

3b. $4.7 − 0.83 =$ _____

3c. $12.17 − 9.49 =$ _____

3d. $16.04 − 5.716 =$ _____

REFLECT

3e.   How can you check a subtraction problem?

_____

_____

3f.   Use the decimals 2.47, 9.57, and 7.1 to write two different addition
facts and two different subtraction facts.

_____

Shade the grid to find each sum.

1. $0.72 + 0.19 = $ _____

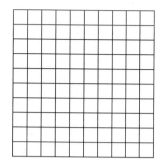

2. $0.38 + 0.4 = $ _____

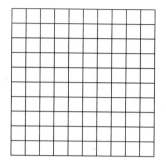

Add or subtract.

3. $54.87 + 7.48 = $ _____

4. $2.19 + 34.92 = $ _____

5. $0.215 + 3.74 = $ _____

6. $28.341 + 37.5 = $ _____

7. $5.623 + 4.19 = $ _____

8. $7.03 + 33.006 = $ _____

9. $0.24 + 1.36 + 7.005 = $ _____

10. $2.25 + 65.47 + 2.333 = $ _____

11. $9.73 - 7.16 = $ _____

12. $18.419 - 6.47 = $ _____

13. $5.006 - 3.2 = $ _____

14. $504.6 - 398.42 = $ _____

15. $25.36 - 2.004 = $ _____

16. $123.8 - 26.42 = $ _____

17. $28.6 - 0.975 = $ _____

18. $5.6 - 0.105 = $ _____

19. $25.68 + 12 = $ _____

20. $57.42 + 4 + 1.602 = $ _____

21. $150.25 - 78 = $ _____

22. $83 - 12.76 = $ _____

Use the café menu to answer each question.

23. What is the cost of a muffin and coffee?

$ \$ $ _____

24. How much more does coffee cost than tea?

$ \$ $ _____

25. Isaac buys 2 bagels. He has a coupon for $1.75 off. How much must Isaac pay? $ \$ $ _____

26. Karen buys a pastry and a cup of tea. She pays with a $10 bill. How much change does she receive?

$ \$ $ _____

Café Menu	
Muffin	$2.79
Bagel	$2.25
Pastry	$3.35
Coffee	$2.50
Tea	$1.79

Multiplying Decimals

Essential question: *How do you multiply decimals?*

COMMON CORE

CC.6.NS.3

1 **EXPLORE** **Modeling Decimal Multiplication**

Use decimal grids or area models to find each product.

A **0.3 × 0.5**

Shade 3 *columns* of the grid to represent 0.3.

Shade _____ *rows* of the grid to represent 0.5.

The shadings overlap _____ square(s).

This represents _____ hundredth(s), or 0.15.

0.3 × 0.5 = _____

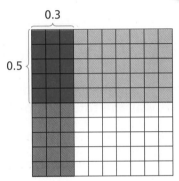

B **3.2 × 2.1**

Each row contains 3 wholes + 2 tenths.

Each column contains _____ whole(s) + _____ tenth(s).

The entire area model represents

_____ whole(s) + _____ tenth(s) + _____ hundredth(s).

3.2 × 2.1 = _____

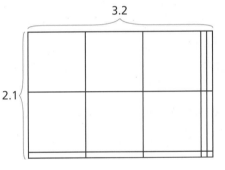

TRY THIS!

1a. Use the grid to multiply 0.3 × 0.8.

1b. Draw an area model to multiply 2.2 × 4.3.

0.3 × 0.8 = _____

2.2 × 4.3 = _____

1c. How are the products 2.1 × 3.2 and 21 × 32 alike? How are they different?

_____

_____

To multiply decimals, first multiply as you would with whole numbers. Then place the decimal point in the product. The number of decimal places in the product equals the sum of the number of decimal places in the factors.

2 EXAMPLE   **Multiplying Decimals**

Dwight bought 2.4 pounds of grapes. The grapes cost $1.95 per pound. What was the total cost of Dwight's grapes?

$$
\begin{array}{r}
1.95 \\
\times\ 2.4 \\
\hline
780 \\
+\ 3900 \\
\hline
4.680
\end{array}
$$

1.95   ←   2 decimal places
× 2.4 ← +   decimal place(s)

4.680 ←   decimal place(s)

The grapes cost $ _____ .

TRY THIS!

Multiply.

2a.

12.6   ←   decimal place(s)

× 15.3 ← +   decimal place(s)

378

+

←   decimal place(s)

2b.

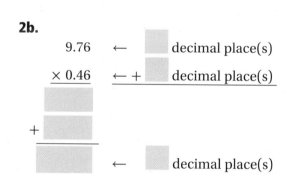

9.76   ←   decimal place(s)

× 0.46 ← +   decimal place(s)

+

←   decimal place(s)

REFLECT

2c. How can you use estimation to check that you have placed the decimal point correctly in your product?

_____

_____

_____

A tree grows 9.25 inches per year. If the tree continues to grow at this rate, how much will the tree grow in 3.75 years?

$$
\begin{array}{r}
9.25 \\
\times\ 3.75 \\
\hline
4625 \\
64750
\end{array}
$$

9.25   ← ☐ decimal place(s)

× 3.75   ← + ☐ decimal place(s)

+ ☐

☐   ← ☐ decimal place(s)

The tree will grow _____ inches in 3.75 years.

Estimate to check whether your answer is reasonable:

Round 9.25 to the nearest whole number. _____

Round 3.75 to the nearest whole number. _____

Multiply the whole numbers. _____

Is the answer reasonable? Explain. _____

TRY THIS!

Multiply.

3a.
$$
\begin{array}{r}
7.14 \\
\times\ 6.78 \\
\hline
5712 \\
\end{array}
$$

+ ☐

3b.
$$
\begin{array}{r}
11.49 \\
\times\ 8.27 \\
\hline
\end{array}
$$

+ ☐

3c. Rico bicycles at an average speed of 15.5 miles per hour. What distance will Rico bicycle in 2.5 hours? _____ miles

3d. Use estimation to show that your answer to **3c** is reasonable.

_____

_____

REFLECT

3e. Compare the products 6.95 × 38.3 and 69.5 × 3.83. What do you notice? Explain.

_____

_____

PRACTICE

1. Use the grid to multiply 0.4×0.7.

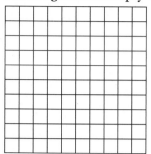

$0.4 \times 0.7 = \underline{\hspace{2cm}}$

2. Draw an area model to multiply 1.1×2.4.

$1.1 \times 2.4 = \underline{\hspace{2cm}}$

Place the decimal point in each product.

3. $3.9 \times 4.6 = 1 \quad 7 \quad 9 \quad 4$

4. $0.219 \times 6.2 = 1 \quad 3 \quad 5 \quad 7 \quad 8$

5. $14.9 \times 0.092 = 1 \quad 3 \quad 7 \quad 0 \quad 8$

6. $5.546 \times 8.14 = 4 \quad 5 \quad 1 \quad 4 \quad 4 \quad 4 \quad 4$

Multiply.

7. $0.18 \times 0.06 = \underline{\hspace{2cm}}$

8. $35.15 \times 3.7 = \underline{\hspace{2cm}}$

9. $0.96 \times 0.12 = \underline{\hspace{2cm}}$

10. $62.19 \times 32.5 = \underline{\hspace{2cm}}$

11. $3.4 \times 4.37 = \underline{\hspace{2cm}}$

12. $3.762 \times 0.66 = \underline{\hspace{2cm}}$

13. $11.89 \times 41 = \underline{\hspace{2cm}}$

14. $73.8 \times 19.85 = \underline{\hspace{2cm}}$

15. $12.7 \times 1.83 = \underline{\hspace{2cm}}$

16. $44.1 \times 24.66 = \underline{\hspace{2cm}}$

17. Chan Hee bought 3.4 pounds of coffee that cost $6.95 per pound. How much did he spend on coffee?

$\underline{\hspace{2.5cm}}

18. Adita earns $9.40 per hour working at an animal shelter. How much money will she earn for 18.5 hours of work?

$\underline{\hspace{2.5cm}}

Catherine tracked her gas purchases for one month.

19. How much did Catherine spend on gas in week 2?

$\underline{\hspace{2.5cm}}

20. How much more did she spend in week 4 than in week 1?

$\underline{\hspace{2.5cm}}

	Gallons	Cost per gallon ($)
Week 1	10.4	2.65
Week 2	11.5	2.54
Week 3	9.72	2.75
Week 4	10.6	2.70

Dividing Decimals

Essential question: *How do you divide decimals?*

COMMON
CORE

CC.6.NS.3

1 E X P L O R E   **Modeling Decimal Division**

Use decimal grids to find each quotient.

A **6.39 ÷ 3**

Shade grids to model 6.39.

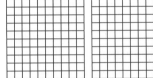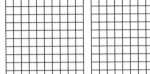

Separate the shaded grids into 3 equal groups. How many are in each group? _____

$6.39 \div 3 =$ _____

B **6.39 ÷ 2.13**

Shade grids to model 6.39.

Separate the model into groups of 2.13. How many groups do you have? _____

$6.39 \div 2.13 =$ _____

TRY THIS!

1a. Use decimal grids to divide $8.48 \div 4$. _____

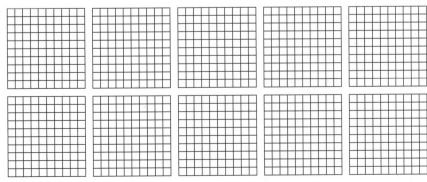

1b. Compare the quotients $6.39 \div 3$ and $639 \div 3$.

_____

_____

1c. When using models to divide decimals, when might you want to use grids divided into tenths instead of hundredths?

_____

_____

Dividing decimals is very similar to dividing whole numbers. When you divide a decimal by a whole number, the placement of the decimal point in the quotient is determined by the placement of the decimal in the dividend.

2 EXAMPLE Dividing Decimals by Whole Numbers

A high school track is 9.76 meters wide. It is divided into 8 lanes of equal width for track and field events. How wide is each lane?

Divide using long division as with whole numbers.

Place a decimal point in the quotient directly above the decimal point in the dividend.

$$\begin{array}{r} 1.\square\square \\ 8)\overline{9.76} \\ -8 \\ \hline 1\,7 \\ -\square\square \\ \hline \square\square \\ -\square\square \\ \hline 0 \end{array}$$

Each lane is _____ meters wide.

TRY THIS!

Divide.

2a. $5)\overline{9.75}$

2b. $7)\overline{6.44}$

REFLECT

2c. How can you estimate to check that your quotient in ② is reasonable?

_____

_____

When dividing a decimal by a decimal, first change the divisor to a whole number by multiplying by a power of 10. Then multiply the dividend by the same power of 10.

3 EXAMPLE Dividing a Decimal by a Decimal

A Ella uses 0.5 pound of raspberries in each raspberry cake that she makes. How many cakes can Ella make with 3.25 pounds of raspberries?

Step 1 The divisor has one decimal place, so multiply both the dividend and the divisor by 10 so that the divisor is a whole number.

$0.5\overline{)3.25}$ $0.5\overline{)3.25}$

$0.5 \times 10 =$ _____

$3.25 \times 10 =$ _____

Step 2 Divide.

$$\begin{array}{r} 6.\quad\ \\ 5\overline{)32.5} \\ -30\ \ \\ \hline 2\ \ \\ -\quad\ \\ \hline \quad \end{array}$$

Ella can make _____ cakes.

B Anthony spent $11.52 for some pens that were on sale for $0.72 each. How many pens did Anthony buy?

Step 1 The divisor has two decimal places, so multiply both the dividend and the divisor by 100 so that the divisor is a whole number.

$0.72\overline{)11.52}$ $0.72\overline{)11.52}$

$0.72 \times 100 =$ _____

$11.52 \times 100 =$ _____

Step 2 Divide.

$$\begin{array}{r} \quad \\ 72\overline{)1152} \\ -72\ \ \\ \hline 4\ \ \\ -\quad \\ \hline \quad \end{array}$$

Anthony bought _____ pens.

TRY THIS!

Divide.

3a. $0.5\overline{)4.25}$

3b. $0.84\overline{)15.12}$

REFLECT

3c. In **A** , the number of batches that Ella can make is not equal to the quotient. Why not?

_____

_____

PRACTICE

Divide.

1. $4\overline{)29.5}$

2. $3.1\overline{)10.261}$

3. $2.4\overline{)16.8}$

4. $0.96\overline{)0.144}$

5. $38.5 \div 0.5 =$ _____

6. $23.85 \div 9 =$ _____

7. $5.6372 \div 0.17 =$ _____

8. $8.19 \div 4.2 =$ _____

9. $66.5 \div 3.5 =$ _____

10. $0.234 \div 0.78 =$ _____

11. $78.74 \div 12.7 =$ _____

12. $36.45 \div 0.09 =$ _____

13. $90 \div 0.36 =$ _____

14. $18.88 \div 1.6 =$ _____

15. Corrine has 9.6 pounds of trail mix to divide into 12 bags. How many pounds of trail mix will go in each bag?   _____ pound(s)

16. Michael paid $11.48 for sliced cheese at the deli counter. The cheese cost $3.28 per pound. How much cheese did Michael buy?   _____ pound(s)

17. A four-person relay team completed a race in 72.4 seconds. On average, what was each runner's time?   _____ second(s)

18. Elizabeth has a piece of ribbon that is 4.5 meters long. She wants to cut it into pieces that are 0.25 meter long. How many pieces of ribbon will she have?   _____ piece(s)

19. Lisa paid $43.95 for 16.1 gallons of gasoline. What was the cost per gallon, rounded to the nearest hundredth? $_____ per gallon

20. One inch is equivalent to 2.54 centimeters. How many inches are there in 50.8 centimeters?   _____ in.

Use the table for 21 and 22.

Custom Printing Costs				
Quantity	25	50	75	100
Mugs	$107.25	$195.51	$261.75	$329.00
T-shirts	$237.50	$441.00	$637.50	$829.00

21. What is the price per mug for 25 coffee mugs? $_____

22. What is the price per T-shirt for 75 T-shirts? $_____

Greatest Common Factor

Essential question: *How do you find and use the greatest common factor of two whole numbers?*

---

1 **EXPLORE** **Greatest Common Factor**

A florist plans to make bouquets of roses and tulips. She has 18 roses and 30 tulips. Each bouquet must have the same number of roses and the same number of tulips. She wants to use all of the flowers. What are the possible bouquets she can make?

A Complete the tables below.

Roses

Number of bouquets	1	2	3	6	9	18
Number of roses in each bouquet	18	9				

Tulips

Number of bouquets	1	2	3	5	6	10	15	30
Number of tulips in each bouquet	30							

B Can the florist make five bouquets? Why or why not?

_____

🔑 If a number is a factor of two or more counting numbers, it is called a *common factor* of those numbers.

C What are the common factors of 18 and 30? What do they represent in this situation?

_____

🔑 The **greatest common factor (GCF)** of two or more counting numbers is the greatest factor shared by the numbers.

D What is the GCF of 18 and 30? _____

If the florist wants the number of bouquets to be as large as possible, how many bouquets can she make? _____

How many roses will be in each bouquet? _____

How many tulips will be in each bouquet? _____

One way to find the GCF of two numbers is to list all of their factors.

2 EXAMPLE Greatest Common Factor

A baker has 24 blueberry muffins and 36 apple muffins to divide into
boxes for sale. Each box must have the same number of blueberry muffins
and the same number of apple muffins. What is the greatest number
of boxes that the baker can make using all of the muffins? How many
blueberry muffins and how many apple muffins will be in each box?

A   List the factors of 24 and 36. Then circle the common factors.

Factors of 24: _____, _____, _____, _____, _____, _____, _____, _____

Factors of 36: _____, _____, _____, _____, _____, _____, _____, _____, _____

B   What do the common factors represent in this situation?

_____

C   What is the GCF of 24 and 36? _____

D   The greatest number of boxes that the baker can make is _____. There will

be _____ blueberry muffin(s) and _____ apple muffin(s) in each box.

TRY THIS!

List the factors to find the GCF of each pair of numbers.

2a.   14 and 35 _____   **2b.**   20 and 28 _____

2c.   The sixth-grade class is competing in the school field day. There are 32 girls and
40 boys who want to participate in the relay race. Each team must have the same number
of girls and the same number of boys. What is the greatest number of teams that can be
formed? How many boys and how many girls will be on each team?

_____

REFLECT

2d.   What is the GCF of two numbers when one number is a multiple of the other?
Give an example.

_____

2e.   What is the GCF of two prime numbers? Give an example.

_____

You can use the Distributive Property to rewrite a sum of two or more numbers as a product of their GCF and another number.

3 **E X P L O R E**   **Distributive Property**

You can use grid paper to draw area models of 45 and 60.
Here are all of the possible area models of 45.

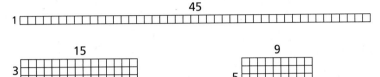

A   What do the side lengths of the area models above (1, 3, 5, 9, 15, and 45) represent? _____

B   On your own grid paper, show all of the possible area models of 60.

C   What side lengths do the area models of 45 and 60 have in common?

_____

What do these side lengths represent? _____

D   What is the greatest common side length? What does it represent?

_____

E   Write 45 as a product of the GCF and another number. _____

Write 60 as a product of the GCF and another number. _____

F   Use your answers above to rewrite 45 + 60.

$45 + 60 = 15 \times \boxed{} + 15 \times \boxed{}$

Use the Distributive Property and your answer above to write 45 + 60 as a product of the GCF and another number.

$15 \times \boxed{} + 15 \times \boxed{} = 15 \times \left(\boxed{} + \boxed{} \right) = 15 \times \boxed{}$

TRY THIS!

Write each sum as a product of the GCF of the two numbers.

3a.   27 + 18 _____   **3b.**   120 + 36 _____

REFLECT

3c.   Does the same process work with subtraction? For example, can you write 120 − 36 as a product of the GCF and another number? Explain.

_____

List the factors of each number.

1. 16 _____

2. 39 _____

3. 50 _____

Find the GCF of each pair of numbers.

4. 40 and 48 _____   **5.** 10 and 45 _____

6. 6 and 21 _____   **7.** 60 and 72 _____

8. 21 and 40 _____   **9.** 28 and 32 _____

10. 28 and 70 _____   **11.** 45 and 81 _____

12. 30 and 45 _____   **13.** 55 and 77 _____

14. Mrs. Davis is sewing vests. She has 16 green buttons and 24 yellow buttons. Each vest will have the same number of yellow buttons and the same number of green buttons. What is the greatest number of vests Mrs. Davis can make using all of the buttons?   _____ vests

15. A baker has 27 wheat bagels and 36 plain bagels that will be divided into boxes. Each box must have the same number of wheat bagels and the same number of plain bagels. What is the greatest number of boxes the baker can make using all of the bagels?   _____ boxes

16. Lola is putting appetizers on plates. She has 63 meatballs and 84 cheese cubes. She wants both kinds of food on each plate, and each plate must have the same number of meatballs and the same number of cheese cubes. What is the greatest number of plates she can make using all of the appetizers?   _____ plates

17. The Delta High School marching band has 54 members. The Swanton High School marching band has 90 members. The bands are going to march in a parade together. The director wants to arrange the bands into the same number of rows. What is the greatest number of rows in which the two bands can be arranged?   _____ rows

Write each sum as a product of the GCF of the two numbers.

18. 75 + 90   **19.** 36 and 45

_____   _____

20. 56 + 64   **21.** 48 + 14

_____   _____

1-7

Least Common Multiple

COMMON CORE

CC.6.NS.4

Essential question: *How do you find the least common multiple of two numbers?*

1 EXPLORE   Least Common Multiple

For the next 100 days, Shannon will be training for a biathlon. She will swim every 6 days and bicycle every 8 days. On what days will she both swim and bicycle?

Step 1 Shade each day Shannon will swim.

Step 2 Circle each day Shannon will bicycle.

1	2	3	4	5	6	7	8	9	10
11	12	13	14	15	16	17	18	19	20
21	22	23	24	25	26	27	28	29	30
31	32	33	34	35	36	37	38	39	40
41	42	43	44	45	46	47	48	49	50
51	52	53	54	55	56	57	58	59	60
61	62	63	64	65	66	67	68	69	70
71	72	73	74	75	76	77	78	79	80
81	82	83	84	85	86	87	88	89	90
91	92	93	94	95	96	97	98	99	100

Shannon will both swim and bicycle on days _____ .

The numbers of the days that Shannon will swim and bicycle are common multiples of 6 and 8.

The **least common multiple (LCM)** is the least common multiple of two or more counting numbers.

What is the LCM of 6 and 8? What does it represent in this situation?

_____

2 EXAMPLE   Least Common Multiple

A store is holding a grand opening promotion. Every 3rd customer receives a free key chain and every 4th customer receives a free magnet. Which customer will be the first to receive both a key chain and a magnet?

List the multiples of each number. Circle the common multiples.

Multiples of 3: _____, _____, _____, _____, _____, _____, _____, _____, _____

Multiples of 4: _____, _____, _____, _____, _____, _____, _____, _____, _____

What is the LCM of 3 and 4? _____

The first customer to get both a key chain and a magnet is _____ .

List multiples to find the LCM of each pair of numbers.

2a. 4 and 9 _____

2b. 18 and 24 _____

REFLECT

2c. What is the LCM of two numbers when one number is a multiple of the other? Give an example.

_____

_____

2d. What is the LCM of two numbers that have no common factors greater than 1? Give an example.

_____

_____

PRACTICE

Find the LCM of each pair of numbers.

1. 6 and 9 _____

2. 9 and 21 _____

3. 8 and 56 _____

4. 16 and 24 _____

5. 12 and 30 _____

6. 6 and 10 _____

7. At a restaurant, after every 12th visit you receive a free beverage. After every 15th visit you receive a free dessert. At which visit will you first receive a free beverage and a free dessert?   Visit _____

8. Starting today (day 1) Lee will walk his dog Fido every 3rd day and his dog Fifi every 5th day. On which day will Lee first walk both dogs together?   Day _____

Use the train schedule for 9 and 10.

9. The red line and the blue line trains just arrived at the station. When will they next arrive at the station at the same time? In _____ minutes

10. All three trains just arrived at the station. When will they next all arrive at the station at the same time? In _____ minutes

Train Schedule	
Train	**Arrives Every...**
Red line	8 minutes
Blue line	10 minutes
Yellow line	12 minutes

Problem Solving Connections

COMMON CORE

CC.6.NS.1
CC.6.NS.2
CC.6.NS.3
CC.6.NS.4

Welcome Back! Elizabeth is an event planner who has been hired to plan a class reunion. The class has 275 people and 256 will be attending. Elizabeth must plan the seating, decorations, and food. She then needs to determine how much to charge each guest so that all costs are covered.

1 Seating

The cost sheet shows the types of tables available, the cost per table, and the cost per tablecloth.

A How many round tables would be necessary to seat all of the guests?

Type of Table	Seats	Cost per Table ($)	Cost per Tablecloth ($)
Round	8	5.00	3.75
Rectangular	12	7.50	4.35

B How many rectangular tables would be necessary to seat all of the guests?

C Which table, round or rectangular, would be cheaper for the reunion? How much cheaper?

D A name card will be placed at each seat. Elizabeth finds that 36 name cards come in a package. How many packages will she need? Explain.

2 Decorations and Favors

A The school colors are blue and white. Elizabeth has 84 blue balloons and 96 white balloons. How many balloon bouquets can she make if she wants to have the same number of each color in each bouquet and use all of her balloons?

B How many of each color balloon will be in each bouquet?

C Elizabeth has 87.75 feet of banner paper. How many banners can she make that are 11.25 feet long? Explain.

D Elizabeth plans to hand out door prizes as the guests arrive. Every 6th guest will receive a mug, and every 14th guest will receive a T-shirt. Which guest will be the first to receive both a mug and a T-shirt?

E Elizabeth has two $8\frac{1}{2}$-pound bags of mints. She plans to put $\frac{1}{12}$ pound at each place setting. Will she have enough mints?

3 Food and Drink

A Use the price sheet to find the total cost of a basic meal of one meat and one side for each guest.

Meal Options	Price per Plate ($)
1 meat, 1 side	9.25
2 meats, 1 side	10.25
Additional sides	0.75
Salad	1.45

B How would you determine how much more it would cost to serve each guest a salad rather than an additional side?

C Elizabeth has budgeted $3,000 for food. If she decides to serve an additional side and a salad, can she choose the meal with two meats and stay within her budget?

D Elizabeth purchases a container of punch mix that, when mixed with water, makes 640 ounces of punch. Elizabeth has 8-ounce drinking glasses. She assumes that each person will drink 2 glasses of punch. Show how to determine how many people can be served with one container of punch.

4 Answer the Question

A Elizabeth's budget for the class reunion is shown. Help her complete the budget using some of your answers from previous questions. You may also have to perform additional computations.

Class Reunion Budget			
Item	Number of Items/Packages	Cost per Item	Total Cost
Rectangular tables		$11.85	
Name cards		$5.10	
Balloons		$0.13	
Sign	1	$25.25	
T-shirts		$7.50	
Mugs		$5.00	
Mints		$5.50	
Meals	256	$11.45	
Punch		$4.25	
Pie	16	$6.75	
Cake	7	$12.00	
Elizabeth's Fee			$1,800.00
Total Cost			

B Based on your total cost, determine the amount each guest should pay to attend the reunion. Would $20 per person be enough to cover all of the expenses? Explain. How much would you charge? Justify your answer.

UNIT 1 TEST PREP

Name _____ Class _____ Date _____

MULTIPLE CHOICE

1. The Harrison family traveled 2,112 miles in four days on their last vacation. The family traveled the same distance each day. How many miles did the Harrisons travel each day?

   A. 506 miles   **C.** 528 miles

   B. 542 miles   **D.** 844 miles

2. Margaret borrowed $2,597 from her parents for a foreign exchange trip. She plans to repay her parents $175 each month. How much will Margaret's last payment be?

   F. $123   **H.** $168

   G. $147   **J.** $175

3. Cedric made 30 cups of soup. How many $1\frac{1}{4}$-cups servings does he have?

   A. 24 servings   **C.** 30 servings

   B. 28 servings   **D.** 35 servings

4. A snail travels 0.03 mile per hour. How far will the snail travel in 36.8 hours?

   F. 0.1104 miles   **H.** 11.04 miles

   G. 1.104 miles   **J.** 110.4 miles

5. A rectangular garden has the dimensions shown in the figure.

   7.48 meters

   15.6 meters

   What is the perimeter of the garden?

   A. 16.24 meters   **C.** 46.16 meters

   B. 23.08 meters   **D.** 116.688 meters

6. Adam drove from his house directly to one of the destinations shown in the table. Adam's trip odometer read 248.9 miles when he left home and 316.3 miles when he reached his destination. What was his destination?

Destination	Distance from Adam's House
Museum	64.6 miles
Baseball stadium	67.4 miles
Theater	70.4 miles
Historical landmark	66.4 miles
Mall	71.4 miles

   F. Mall

   G. Theater

   H. Historical landmark

   J. Baseball stadium

7. Rusty has $25.45 in the bank and $16.18 in his wallet. He wants to purchase a sweater that costs $49.99. How much more money does he need?

   A. $41.63   **C.** $24.54

   B. $33.81   **D.** $8.36

8. Josie has $24\frac{1}{2}$ pounds of birdseed. She puts $1\frac{3}{4}$ pounds of seed in her feeders each day. How many days will she be able to fill her feeders?

   F. $10\frac{1}{2}$ days   **H.** 16 days

   G. 14 days   **J.** $18\frac{1}{2}$ days

9. Which of the following quotients has the greatest value?

   A. $0.075 \div 6$ **C.** $0.75 \div 0.06$

   B. $7.5 \div 0.006$ **D.** $0.75 \div 0.6$

10. For a soccer clinic, 15 coaches and 35 players will be split into groups. Each group must have the same number of players and the same number of coaches. At most, how many groups can there be?

F. 3 groups   H. 7 groups

G. 5 groups   J. 15 groups

11. Two cruise ships set sail from Florida on the same day. One makes a round trip every 12 days, and the other makes a round trip every 16 days. In how many days will both cruise ships be in Florida again?

A. 32 days   C. 48 days

B. 40 days   D. 192 days

FREE RESPONSE

12. You deposited $45.25 in your checking account, but instead of adding $45.25 to your balance, the bank accidentally subtracted $45.25. How much money should the bank add to your account to correct the mistake? Explain.

_____

_____

_____

_____

13. Is the quotient 4.5 ÷ 0.9 greater or less than 4.5? Why?

_____

_____

_____

14. The greatest common factor of 18 and a mystery number is 6. Give three possible values for the mystery number.

_____

15. Apples cost $1.29 per pound. How much would a bag of apples weighing 4.7 pounds cost? (Round your answer to the nearest cent.)

_____

16. A bridge is 21.6 kilometers long. A nearby tunnel is 2.3 times as long as the bridge. How long is the tunnel?

_____

17. Explain how to draw a model to find the quotient of 2.4 ÷ 3. What is this quotient?

_____

_____

_____

_____

_____

18. What is the least number that has both 6 and 10 as factors?

_____

19. Tyler has a piece of ribbon that is $\frac{3}{4}$ yard long. How many $\frac{1}{8}$-yard pieces can he cut? Draw and label a diagram to support your answer.

_____

The Number System: Positive and Negative Numbers

Unit Focus

You have learned that integers are the set of whole numbers and their opposites. In this unit, you will learn more about integers as well as other positive and negative rational numbers. You will learn real-world applications of positive and negative numbers, such as temperatures above and below 0. You will compare and order positive and negative numbers, and you will learn about opposites and absolute value. Finally, you will learn about the coordinate plane and how to find the distance between two points in the coordinate plane.

Unit at a Glance

COMMON CORE

UNIT 2

Unpacking the Common Core State Standards

Use the table to help you understand the Standards for Mathematical Content that are taught in this unit. Refer to the lessons listed after each standard for exploration and practice.

COMMON CORE Standards for Mathematical Content	What It Means For You
CC.6.NS.5 Understand that positive and negative numbers are used together to describe quantities having opposite directions or values; use positive and negative numbers...in real-world contexts... Lesson 2-1	You will represent positive and negative numbers on a number line and use them to describe situations in the real world, such as temperatures above and below 0.
CC.6.NS.6a Recognize opposite signs of numbers as indicating locations on opposite sides of 0 on the number line; recognize that the opposite of the opposite of a number is the number itself... Lesson 2-1	You will learn that numbers with opposite signs (+ and –) are located on opposite sides of 0 on the number line. You will identify the opposite of a number.
CC.6.NS.6b Understand signs of numbers in ordered pairs as indicating quadrants of the coordinate plane... Lesson 2-4	You will learn to graph ordered pairs of positive and negative numbers on the coordinate plane and identify the quadrant in which a point is located.
CC.6.NS.6c Find and position...rational numbers on a ...number line diagram; find and position pairs of ...rational numbers on a coordinate plane. Lessons 2-1, 2-4	You will use a number line to order a set of positive and negative numbers. You will graph an ordered pair of rational numbers in a coordinate plane.
CC.6.NS.7a Interpret statements of inequality as statements about the relative position of two numbers on a number line. Lesson 2-2	You will learn the relative positions on a number line of two unequal numbers. You will also learn how to write a statement of inequality.
CC.6.NS.7b Write, interpret, and explain statements of order for rational numbers in real-world contexts. Lesson 2-2	You will use your knowledge of rational numbers to describe and explain real-world situations.
CC.6.NS.7c Understand absolute value of a rational number as its distance from 0 on the number line... Lesson 2-3	You will learn that absolute value is a distance on the number line. You will apply absolute value to real-world situations.
CC.6.NS.8 Solve...problems by graphing points in all four quadrants of the coordinate plane. Lesson 2-4	You will graph points on the coordinate plane to solve real-world and mathematical problems.

UNIT 2

The Number Line

COMMON CORE

CC.6.NS.5
CC.6.NS.6a
CC.6.NS.6c

Essential question: *How are positive and negative numbers represented on a number line?*

Positive numbers are numbers greater than 0. They are located to the right of 0 on a number line. Positive numbers can be written with or without a plus sign; for example, 3 is the same as +3.

Negative numbers are numbers less than 0. They are located to the left of 0 on a number line. Negative numbers must always be written with a negative sign.

The number 0 is neither positive nor negative.

1 EXPLORE Positive and Negative Numbers

The elevation of a location describes its height above or below sea level, which has elevation 0. Elevations below sea level are represented by negative numbers, and elevations above sea level are represented by positive numbers.

A   The table shows the elevations of several locations in a state park.
Graph the locations on the number line according to their elevations.

Location	Little Butte A	Cradle Creek B	Dinosaur Valley C	Mesa Ridge D	Juniper Trail E
Elevation (ft)	5	−5	−8.5	8	−3

B   What point on the number line represents sea level? _____

C   Which location is closest to sea level? How do you know?

_____

D   Is the location in C above or below sea level? _____

E   Which two locations are the same distance from sea level? Are these locations above or below sea level?

_____

F   Which location has the least elevation? How do you know?

_____

TRY THIS!

1. The table shows winter temperatures of several world cities. Graph the cities on the number line according to their temperatures.

City	Anchorage, AK, USA F	Fargo, ND, USA G	Oslo, Norway H	St. Petersburg, Russia I	Helsinki, Finland J	Budapest, Hungary K
Temperature (°F)	−4	9	−6	−10	7	6

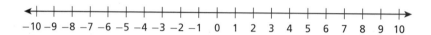

Two numbers are **opposites** if, on a number line, they are the same distance from 0 but on different sides of 0. For example, 5 and −5 are opposites; 2.15 and −2.15 are also opposites. 0 is its own opposite.

Integers are the set of all whole numbers and their opposites.

2 EXPLORE **Opposites**

On graph paper, use a ruler or straightedge to draw a number line. Label the number line with each integer from −10 to 10. Fold your number line in half so that the crease goes through 0. Numbers that line up after folding the number line are opposites.

A Use your number line to find the opposites of 7, −4, 1, and 9. _____

B How does your number line show that 0 is its own opposite?

_____

C What is the opposite of 8.5? _____

D What is the opposite of the opposite of 3? _____

TRY THIS!

2a. Graph and label the following points on the number line.

A. −2   **B.** 9.5   **C.** −8   **D.** −9.5   **E.** 5   **F.** 8

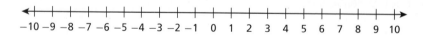

2b. Which points represent integers? _____

2c. Which pairs of points represent opposites? _____

Comparing and Ordering Numbers

COMMON
CORE

CC.6.NS.7a
CC.6.NS.7b

Essential question: *How do you compare and order positive and negative numbers?*

---

1 **EXPLORE** **Comparing Positive and Negative Integers**

The Westfield soccer league ranks its teams using a number called the "win/loss combined record." A team with more wins than losses will have a positive combined record, and a team with fewer wins than losses will have a negative combined record. The table shows the total win/loss combined record for each team at the end of the season.

Team	Sharks A	Jaguars B	Badgers C	Tigers D	Cougars E	Hawks F	Wolves G
Win/Loss Combined Record	−4	3	−7	−8	−1	−5	7

A On the number line, graph a point for each team according to its win/loss combined record.

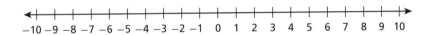

B Which team had the best record in the league? How do you know?

_____

_____

C Which team had the worst record? How do you know?

_____

_____

REFLECT

1. How would you evaluate the Westfield league as a whole? Explain.

_____

_____

_____

When you read a number line from left to right, the numbers are in order from least to greatest.

Graph the following rational numbers on the number line:

1.6   3.8   4.9   2.0   5.3   −1.2

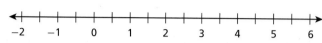

To list the numbers in order from least to greatest, read the numbers on the number line from left to right.

_____

A   Which number is third least? _____

B   Which number is second greatest? _____

TRY THIS!

Graph each set of numbers on a number line. Then list the numbers in order from least to greatest.

2a.   5.6   −8   3.1   −4   7   −2

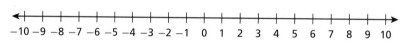

_____

2b.   −14   12   −7   11   18   −2   1   5   −8

_____

REFLECT

2c.   In a given list of numbers, the greatest number is negative. What can you say about the numbers in this list?

_____

An **inequality** is a statement that two quantities are not equal. The symbols < and > are used to write inequalities.

- The symbol > means "is greater than."
- The symbol < means "is less than."

You can use a number line to help write an inequality.

On December 18, the high temperature in Portland, Oregon, was 42 °F.
On January 18, the high temperature was 28 °F. Which day was warmer?

Graph 42 and 28 on the number line.

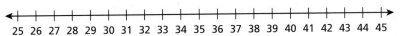

25 26 27 28 29 30 31 32 33 34 35 36 37 38 39 40 41 42 43 44 45

A   42 is to the right of 28 on the number line.

This means that 42 is greater than / less than 28.

Use < or > to complete the inequality: 42 ☐ 28.

B   28 is to the left of 42 on the number line.

This means that 28 is greater than / less than 42.

Use < or > to complete the inequality: 28 ☐ 42.

The temperature was warmer on _____.

C   In **A** and **B** , you wrote two inequalities to compare 42 and 28.
Write two inequalities to compare −6 and 7. _____

D   Write two inequalities to compare −9 and −4. _____

TRY THIS!

Compare. Write > or <. Use the number line to help you, if necessary.

3a. −10 ☐ −2   **3b.** −6 ☐ 6   **3c.** −7.1 ☐ −8.3

−10 −9 −8 −7 −6 −5 −4 −3 −2 −1 0 1 2 3 4 5 6 7 8 9 10

3d. Write two inequalities to compare −2 and −18. _____

3e. Write two inequalities to compare 39 and −39. _____

REFLECT

3f. Negative numbers are _____ than positive numbers.

3g. 0 is _____ than all negative numbers.

3h. What is the greatest negative integer? _____

3i. Is there a greatest positive integer? If so, what is it? If not, why not?

_____

_____

3j. What is the least nonnegative number? _____

PRACTICE

1a. On the number line, graph a point for each of the following cities according to their temperatures.

City	A	B	C	D	E
Temperature (°F)	−9	10	−2	0	4

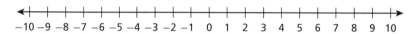

b. Which city was coldest? _____

c. Which city was warmest? _____

List the numbers in order from least to greatest.

2. 4, −6, 0, 8, −9, 1, −3

_____

3. 31, 5, 7, −0.1, 1, 1.5, −9

_____

4. −80, 88, 96, −14, 75, 59, −32

_____

5. −65, 34, 7.6, −13, 55, 62.5, −7.6

_____

6. Write two inequalities to compare −17 and −22. _____

7. Write two inequalities to compare 16 and −2. _____

Compare. Write < or >.

8. 9 ⬚ 2

9. 0 ⬚ 6

10. 3 ⬚ −7

11. 5 ⬚ −10

12. −1 ⬚ −3

13. -8 ⬚ −4

14. −4.5 ⬚ 1

15. −2 ⬚ −2.5

16. Which costs more, a fruit cup or veggies and dip? Use the given prices to write an inequality that shows your answer.

_____

Fruit cup	$2.49
Veggies and dip	$2.86
Yogurt	$1.97
Fruit smoothie	$3.83
Pretzels	$1.71

17. Which costs less, pretzels or yogurt? Use the given prices to write an inequality that shows your answer.

_____

18. Error Analysis At 9:00 P.M., the outside temperature was −3 °F. The newscaster says that the temperature will be −12 °F by midnight. Bethany says, "It will be warmer outside by midnight." Why is Bethany incorrect?

_____

Absolute Value

COMMON
CORE

CC.6.NS.7c
CC.6.NS.7d

Essential question: *How do you find and use absolute value?*

The **absolute value** of a number is the number's distance from 0 on the number line. For example, the absolute value of -3 is 3 because -3 is 3 units from 0. The absolute value of -3 is written $|-3|$.

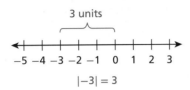

$|-3| = 3$

Because absolute value represents a distance, it is always nonnegative.

1 EXPLORE   Finding Absolute Value

Graph the following numbers on the number line. Then use your number line to find each absolute value.

$$-7 \qquad 5 \qquad 7 \qquad -2 \qquad 4 \qquad -4$$

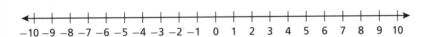

A $|-7| =$ _____   **B** $|5| =$ _____   **C** $|7| =$ _____

D $|-2| =$ _____   **E** $|4| =$ _____   **F** $|-4| =$ _____

REFLECT

1a. Which pairs of numbers have the same absolute value? How are these numbers related?

_____

1b. Do you think a number's absolute value can be 0? If so, which number(s) have an absolute value of 0? If not, explain.

_____

1c. If a number is _____, then the number is equal to its absolute value. If a number is _____, then the number is less than its absolute value.

1d. Negative numbers are less than positive numbers. Does this mean that the absolute value of a negative number must be less than the absolute value of a positive number? Explain.

_____

_____

In real-world situations, absolute values are often used instead of negative numbers. For example, if Susan charges a total of $25 on her credit card, we can say that Susan has a balance of −$25. However, we usually say that Susan owes $25.

2 EXPLORE   **Comparing Absolute Values**

Maria, Susan, George, and Antonio received their credit card statements. The amounts owed are shown.

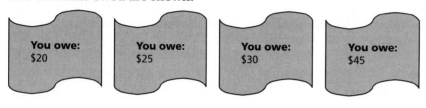

| You owe: | You owe: | You owe: | You owe: |
| $20 | $25 | $30 | $45 |

_____   _____   _____   _____

Answer the following questions. When you have finished, you will have enough clues to match each statement with the correct person.

Remember: When someone owes a positive amount of money, this means that he or she has a *negative* balance.

A Maria's credit card balance is less than −$30. Does Maria owe more than $30 or less than $30? _____

B Susan's credit card balance is greater than −$25. Does Susan owe more than $25 or less than $25? _____

C George's credit card balance is $5 less than Susan's balance. Does George owe more than Susan or less than Susan? _____

D Antonio owes $15 less than Maria owes. This means that Antonio's balance is _____ than Maria's balance.

E Write each person's name underneath his or her credit card statement.

REFLECT

2. Use absolute value to describe the relationship between a negative credit card balance and the amount owed.

_____

The Coordinate Plane

COMMON
CORE

CC.6.NS.6b
CC.6.NS.6c
CC.6.NS.8

Essential question: *How do you locate and name points in the coordinate plane?*

A **coordinate plane** is formed by two number lines that intersect at right angles. The point of intersection is the 0 on each number line.

- The two number lines are called the **axes**.
- The horizontal axis is called the **x-axis**.
- The vertical axis is called the **y-axis**.
- The point where the axes intersect is called the **origin**.
- The two axes divide the coordinate plane into four **quadrants**.

An **ordered pair** is a pair of numbers that gives the location of a point on a coordinate plane. The first number tells how far to the right (positive) or left (negative) the point is located from the origin. The second number tells how far up (positive) or down (negative) the point is located from the origin.

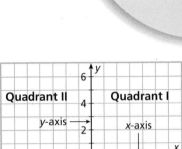
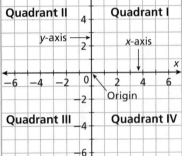

The numbers in an ordered pair are called **coordinates**. The first number is the **x-coordinate** and the second number is the **y-coordinate**.

1 EXAMPLE   Identifying Coordinates and Quadrants

Identify the coordinates of point *D* and name the quadrant where the point is located.

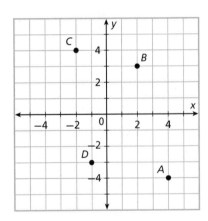

Step 1 Start at the origin. Count horizontally along the *x*-axis until you are directly above point *D*.

How many units did you count? _____

Did you move left (negative) or right (positive) from the origin? _____

The *x*-coordinate of *D* is _____

Step 2 Now count vertically until you reach point *D*.

How many units did you count? _____

Did you move up (positive) or down (negative)? _____

The *y*-coordinate of *D* is _____

The coordinates of *D* are $\left(\boxed{}, \boxed{}\right)$.

D is in Quadrant $\boxed{}$.

Identify the coordinates of each point in the coordinate plane and name the quadrant where each point is located.

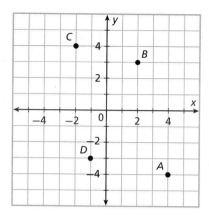

1a. A _____

1b. B _____

1c. If both coordinates of a point are negative, in which quadrant is the point located? _____

1d. Describe the coordinates of all points in Quadrant I.

_____

Points that are located on the axes are not located in any quadrant. Points on the x-axis have a y-coordinate of 0, and points on the y-axis have an x-coordinate of 0.

2 EXAMPLE   Graphing Points on the Coordinate Plane

Leonardo and Christie walk to school each morning. They pass a post office, a coffee shop, and a church on the way. After school, they often study at the library or meet friends at an arcade before walking home.

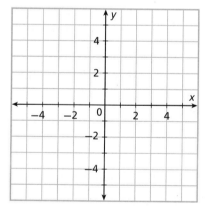

The coordinate plane represents a map of Leonardo and Christie's town. The post office is located at (0, 3). Graph and label this location on the coordinate plane.

Start at the origin.

The first coordinate of the ordered pair tells how many units to move left or right. How many units will you move?

_____

The second coordinate of the ordered pair tells how many units to move up or down. How many units will you move? _____

Will you move up or down? How do you know? _____

The point that represents the post office is located on the _____.

Graph and label each location on the coordinate plane.

2a. Home: $(-4, 2)$ **2b.** Coffee shop: $(3, 2)$ **2c.** Church: $(5, -2)$

2d. School: $(4, -5)$ **2e.** Library: $(-4, -5)$ **2f.** Arcade: $(-2, 0)$

2g. What are the coordinates of the origin? _____

Draw a coordinate plane on graph paper. Label both axes from −10 to 10.

A Graph (3, −2). Then fold your coordinate plane along the y-axis and find the reflection of (3, −2). (Hold the paper up to the light if necessary.)

When (3, −2) is reflected across the y-axis, the coordinates of the new

point are (⬚ , ⬚).

B Unfold your coordinate plane. Then fold it along the x-axis and find the reflection of (3, −2).

When (3, −2) is reflected across the x-axis, the coordinates of the new

point are (⬚ , ⬚).

C Choose four additional points and repeat the steps in **A** and **B**.

Point	Reflected across y-axis	Reflected across x-axis

REFLECT

3a. What is the relationship between the coordinates of a point and the coordinates of its reflection across each axis?

_____

_____

3b. A point in Quadrant II is reflected across the x-axis. The new point is located in Quadrant _____ .

3c. A point in Quadrant _____ is reflected across the y-axis. The new point is located in Quadrant II.

3d. **Conjecture** A point is reflected across the y-axis. Then the reflected point is reflected across the x-axis. How will the coordinates of the final point be related to the coordinates of the original point?

_____

_____

PRACTICE

Use the coordinate plane for 1–10.

Identify the coordinates of each point and name the quadrant in which it is located.

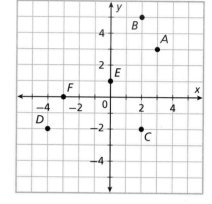

1. A _____

2. B _____

3. C _____

4. D _____

5. E _____

6. F _____

Graph each point on the coordinate plane.

7. $(2, -4)$

8. $(-4, 4)$

9. $(3, 0)$

10. $(0, -5)$

11. Circle the point(s) located in Quadrant III.

$(6, 4)$ $(-5, -1)$ $(3.5, -7)$ $(-1, 0)$ $(-2, -4)$ $(-2, 9.1)$

12. **a.** Choose a point located in Quadrant IV and give its coordinates.

_____

   b. Choose a point that is not located in any quadrant and give its coordinates.

_____

13. The September game schedule for Justin's soccer team is shown. The location of each game is graphed on the coordinate plane.

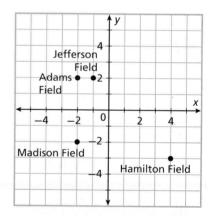

Hawks' Game Schedule
September
Sept 3 – Hawks vs. Jets, Jefferson Field
Sept 10 – Hawks vs. Mustangs, Madison Field
Sept 17 – Hawks vs. Lions, Hamilton Field
Sept 24 – Hawks vs. Arrows, Adams Field

   a. Identify the coordinates of each location.

   Jefferson Field _____   Madison Field _____

   Hamilton Field _____   Adams Field _____

   b. On October 1, the team has a game scheduled at Lincoln Field. The coordinates for Lincoln Field are $(4, 4)$. Graph and label this point on the coordinate plane. What quadrant is Lincoln Field located in? _____

Distance in the Coordinate Plane

COMMON
CORE

CC.6.NS.8

Essential question: *How do you find the distance between two points in the coordinate plane?*

1 **EXPLORE** **Distance in the Coordinate Plane**

A Graph and label the following points on the coordinate plane.

$A(4, 3)$ $B(-4, 4)$ $C(-4, -2)$ $D(1, -2)$

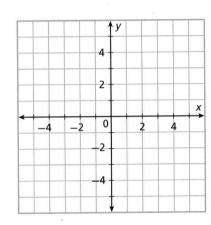

B Count the number of units between *B* and *C*.

The distance between *B* and *C* is _____ units.

C Count the number of units between *C* and *D*.

The distance between *C* and *D* is _____ units.

TRY THIS!

Use the coordinate plane to answer the following questions.

1a. What are the coordinates of point *P*? _____

1b. What are the coordinates of point *Q*? _____

1c. What is the distance between *P* and *Q*? _____ units

1d. What is the distance between $(-4, -4)$ and $(-4, 7)$?

_____ units

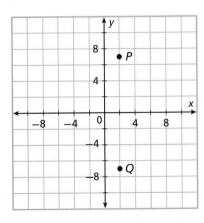

EXPLORE **Solving Distance Problems**

The coordinate plane represents a map. Each grid unit represents one mile. A retail company has warehouses at $M(-7, 1)$ and $N(5, 1)$. The company also has two stores along the straight road between the two warehouses.

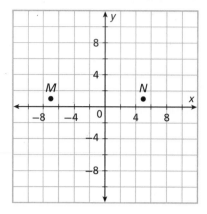

A What is the distance between the warehouses?

_____

Each store is the same distance from a warehouse. Also, the distance between the stores is half the distance between the warehouses. The nearest warehouse to store 1 is warehouse M, and the nearest warehouse to store 2 is warehouse N.

B What is the distance between the two stores?

_____

C What are the coordinates of store 1's location? Graph and label this point on the map. What is the distance from store 1 to the nearest warehouse?

_____

D What are the coordinates of store 2's location? Graph and label this point on the map. What is the distance from store 2 to the nearest warehouse?

_____

REFLECT

2. Check that your answers match the information given in the problem.

Is each store the same distance from a warehouse?   Yes / No

Is the distance between the stores half the distance
between the warehouses?   Yes / No

Is warehouse M the nearest warehouse to store 1?   Yes / No

Is warehouse N the nearest warehouse to store 2?   Yes / No

Problem Solving Connections

Treasure Hunt Carlos has heard stories about buried treasure near his hometown. According to local legend, a pirate buried his treasure, drew a map, and hid clues at various locations. He planned to reclaim his treasure one day, but never returned, and the map, clues, and treasure have never been found. Recently, Carlos bought an old map at an antique store. Could this be the legendary treasure map?

COMMON CORE

CC.6.NS.6b,
CC.6.NS .6c,
CC.6.NS.7a,
CC.6.NS.7b,
CC.6.NS.8

1 Locations in a Coordinate Plane

A Carlos copies the old map onto a coordinate plane. Directions on the back of the map describe distances in steps, so Carlos measures the length of his step and sizes his grid so that each unit represents 1 step.

The starting point on the original map corresponds to $(-5, -4)$ on Carlos's copy of the map. Graph this point on the coordinate plane and label it "Start".

B Carlos reads the back of the original map.

> 1. FROM THE START:
>   15 STEPS NORTH
>   THEN 15 STEPS EAST
>   LARGE CRACK IN NEARBY ROCK

What are the coordinates of Carlos's location after he follows the directions?

_____

Graph this point on the coordinate plane and label it "Rock".

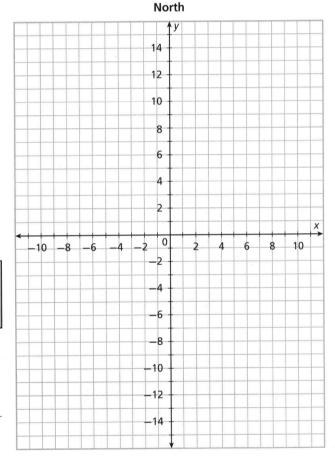

C Carlos finds an old piece of paper inside the rock and follows the directions on it.

> 2. 6 STEPS WEST, THEN 16 SOUTH
>   UNDER THE ROOTS OF AN OLD TREE

What are the coordinates of Carlos's new location? _____

Graph this point on the coordinate plane and label it "Tree".

2 Distance in a Coordinate Plane

A Carlos measured his step length as 3 feet. How many steps has Carlos walked so far? What is this distance in feet?

B Under a tree root, Carlos finds a second map. This map shows a church, a well, and a dry creek bed. Carlos graphs these locations on his copy of the first map as shown.

Give the coordinates of each location.

Church _____

Well _____

Dry creek bed _____

North

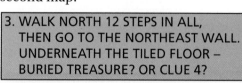

C How far is the dry creek bed from the church?

_____ steps, or _____ feet

How far is the church from the well?

_____ steps, or _____ feet

D Carlos finds these directions written on the back of the second map.

> 3. WALK NORTH 12 STEPS IN ALL,
> THEN GO TO THE NORTHEAST WALL.
> UNDERNEATH THE TILED FLOOR –
> BURIED TREASURE? OR CLUE 4?

Carlos walks 12 steps north to find the ruins of an old church.

How many steps has Carlos walked from the starting point to the church? What is this distance in feet?

E The crafty old pirate has sent Carlos on a long winding route to the old church. Find a shorter path from Carlos's starting point to the church, assuming that Carlos can walk only north, south, east, or west. Draw your path on the coordinate plane.

Describe how to follow your path from the starting point, and find the distance in steps and in feet.

_____

_____

_____

_____

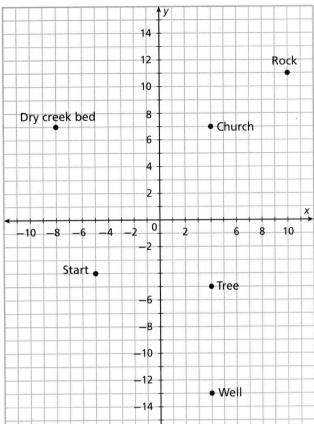

3 Comparing and Ordering

A The church's roof has collapsed and the tile floor is cracked. Carlos locates the northeast wall and begins to dig. Soon he uncovers an old wooden chest. Has he found the treasure?

Carlos opens the chest and finds... several rocks and another piece of paper.

> 4. CASTLE ISLAND'S *EGHHIST INOPT*
>   AT THE TOP, USE YER SCOPE.
>   LOOK TO THE SOUTH.
>   GO TO THE PLACE YOU SEE
>   AND FIND ITS MOUTH.

Carlos knows that Castle Island is nearby, but he does not fully understand the clue. Two of the words are scrambled. Carlos turns the paper over and finds a table:

T	O	N	P	T	H	S	I	G	H	E	I
0	5	10	3	12	−9	−1	8	−6	−4	−2	−7

To unscramble the words, first write the numbers in the table in order from least to greatest.

_____

Now replace each number in your list with the corresponding letter from the table.

The scrambled words are _____.

B When Carlos arrives at Castle Island, he sees this sign.

> **WELCOME TO CASTLE ISLAND!**
> Bilge Basin, Elev. −6 ft →
> ← Buccaneer Beach, Elev. 0 ft
> Galley Ridge, Elev. 509 ft ↗
> ↖ Pirate's Peak, Elev. 628 ft
> Polly's Park, Elev. 128 ft ↗

List the locations on the sign in order from the least elevation to the greatest elevation.

_____

_____

The highest point on Castle Island is _____.

Its elevation is _____ feet.

C From the island's highest point, Carlos looks south through his binoculars and sees a small remote beach.

Write an integer to describe Carlos's descent to this beach. (Assume that the beach is at sea level.) _____

D On the beach, there is an old wooden sign with faded letters. Carlos can barely read *Captain's Cave, Elev. −3 ft.* He sees the opening of a cave nearby. Could this be the beach's "mouth" described in Clue 4?

Is Captain's Cave above or below sea level? _____

Write an inequality using the elevations to justify your answer.

_____

Is Captain's Cave higher or lower than Bilge Basin? _____

Write an inequality using their elevations to justify your answer.

_____

E At the back of the cave, Carlos moves several large loose rocks to reveal a small recess in the cave wall. He reaches in and pries out another old wooden chest, similar to the one he found at the church. Is this the treasure at last?

Carlos slowly opens the lid and...

IT'S THE TREASURE!!!!

To find the treasure's value, first rearrange the numbers in the table in order from least to greatest. Then replace each number with its corresponding letter.

The treasure has _____ value!

2	−9	5	−6	−1	9	0	−4
U	A	T	B	O	E	L	S

Name _____ Class _____ Date _____

MULTIPLE CHOICE

1. Which list of numbers is in order from least to greatest?

   A. −0.8, 1.2, −19, 13, 16, −4, 25

   B. −1, −4, −8, 1.1, 1.6, −19, 23

   C. −19, −8, −4, −1, 1.1, 1.6, 2.5

   D. −1, −4, 1.1, 1.3, 16, −19, 25

2. Which of the following numbers is the opposite of −37?

   F. −73   **H.** 37

   G. −37   **J.** 73

3. What is the absolute value of 45?

   A. −45   **C.** 0.45

   B. 0   **D.** 45

4. Both coordinates of a point in the coordinate plane are negative. In which quadrant is this point located?

   F. Quadrant I   **H.** Quadrant III

   G. Quadrant II   **J.** Quadrant IV

5. Which of the points on the coordinate plane has coordinates (−7, 4)?

   A. A   **C.** C

   B. B   **D.** D

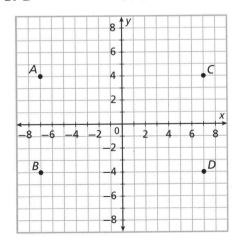

6. Which of the following inequalities is a true statement?

   F. 37 > 73   **H.** 73 < 37

   G. 48 > 24   **J.** 24 > 48

7. Which of the following numbers is located to the right of −47 on the number line?

   A. −14   **C.** −49

   B. −94   **D.** −57

8. The elevation of the Dead Sea is about 1,310 feet below sea level. Which integer represents this elevation?

   F. −1,310   **H.** 131

   G. −131   **J.** 1,310

9. Which of the following coordinates is farthest to the right of the origin on a coordinate plane?

   A. (−19, 7)   **C.** (4, 15)

   B. (0, 12)   **D.** (7, 0)

10. The table shows the low temperature for several days. Which day was the coldest?

Day	Temperature (°F)
Monday	−4
Tuesday	0
Wednesday	−2
Thursday	5
Friday	3

   F. Monday

   G. Tuesday

   H. Wednesday

   J. Thursday

11. Which point is not located in a quadrant?

    A. $(1, -2)$

    B. $(-2.5, 3)$

    C. $(5, 0)$

    D. $(-6, -10)$

12. The point $(-2, -2)$ is reflected across the x-axis. What are the coordinates of the new point?

    F. $(-2, -2)$ **H.** $(2, -2)$

    G. $(-2, 2)$ **J.** $(2, 2)$

13. Which statement about negative numbers is **not** true?

    A. Negative numbers are located to the left of 0 on a number line.

    B. The absolute value of a negative number is negative.

    C. Negative numbers are less than positive numbers.

    D. A negative number is less than its opposite.

14. What is the opposite of the opposite of -7?

    F. -7 **H.** $|7|$

    G. 7 **J.** $|-7|$

FREE RESPONSE

Use the number line for 15–17.

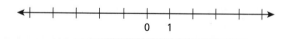

15. The number line has been partially labeled. Label the rest of the number line.

16. Graph the integers $-2, 4, 1$, and their opposites on the number line.

17. Choose one of the integers from item 16 and show on the number line how to find its absolute value.

Mark drives to work every morning. On the way, he stops for breakfast at a café. His route is mapped on the coordinate plane.

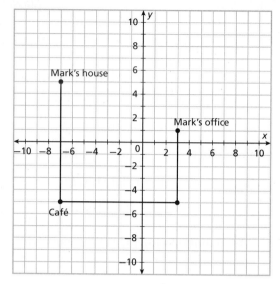

18. Each unit on the coordinate plane represents 1 mile. What is the distance from Mark's house to the café?

_____

19. What is the total distance that Mark drives to work?

_____

20. Will walks his dog at a local park every day after school.

    a. The park is located at $(-4, -3)$ on the map. Graph and label this point.

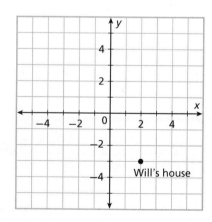

    b. Each unit on the coordinate plane represents 1 block. What is the distance from Will's house to the park in blocks?

_____

Expressions

Unit Focus

In this unit, you will write algebraic expressions that contain variables and constants. You will evaluate expressions and work with equivalent expressions.

Unit at a Glance

COMMON
CORE

UNIT 3

Unpacking the Common Core State Standards

Use the table to help you understand the Standards for Mathematical Content that are taught in this unit. Refer to the lessons listed after each standard for exploration and practice.

COMMON CORE Standards for Mathematical Content	What It Means For You
CC.6.EE.1 Write and evaluate numerical expressions involving whole-number exponents. Lesson 3-1	You will use exponents to show repeated multiplication.
CC.6.EE.2a Write expressions that record operations with numbers and with letters standing for numbers. Lesson 3-2	You will write algebraic expressions containing variables to stand for numbers that are not yet known.
CC.6.EE.2b Identify parts of an expression using mathematical terms (sum, term, product, factor, quotient, coefficient); view one or more parts of an expression as a single entity. Lesson 3-3	You will describe expressions and their parts using words such as sum, term, product, factor, quotient, and coefficient.
CC.6.EE.2c Evaluate expressions at specific values of their variables. Include expressions that arise from formulas used in real-world problems. Perform arithmetic operations, including those involving whole-number exponents, in the conventional order when there are no parentheses to specify a particular order. (Order of Operations) Lesson 3-4	You will identify variables in expressions, including expressions that represent real-world problems. You will learn the order in which to perform arithmetic operations.
CC.6.EE.3 Apply the properties of operations to generate equivalent expressions. Lesson 3-5	Given an algebraic expression, you will write equivalent expressions.
CC.6.EE.4 Identify when two expressions are equivalent (i.e., when the two expressions name the same number regardless of which value is substituted into them). Lesson 3-5	You will identify equivalent expressions.
CC.6.EE.6 Use variables to represent numbers and write expressions when solving a real-world or mathematical problem; understand that a variable can represent an unknown number, or, depending on the purpose at hand, any number in a specified set. Lesson 3-2	You will learn to write algebraic expressions to represent real-world and mathematical problems.

UNIT 3

Exponents

Essential question: *How do you use exponents to represent numbers?*

COMMON
CORE

CC.6.EE.1

1 **E X P L O R E** Exponents

Ricardo observed the hourly growth of bacteria in a test tube and recorded his observations in a table.

Time (h)	Total Bacteria
0	1
1	2
2	$2 \times 2 =$
3	$2 \times 2 \times 2 =$
4	$2 \times 2 \times 2 \times 2 =$

A Complete the table. What pattern(s) do you see in the Total Bacteria column?

_____

B At 2 hours, the total is equal to the product of two 2's.

At 3 hours, the total is equal to the product of _____ 2's.

At 4 hours, the total is equal to the product of _____ 2's.

To show a number multiplied by itself, you can write a *power*. A **power** is an expression with an *exponent* and a *base*. For example, 7^3 means the product of three 7's:

$$7^3 = 7 \times 7 \times 7 = 343$$

The **base** is the number that is multiplied.

The **exponent** tells how many times the base appears in the product.

TRY THIS!

Circle the base.

1a. 4^7 **1b.** 3^5 **1c.** 2^5 **1d.** $\left(\frac{1}{5}\right)^3$

Circle the exponent.

1e. 6^2 **1f.** 10^6 **1g.** $\left(\frac{7}{10}\right)^8$ **1h.** 9^4

1i. **Conjecture** What do you think it means to have an exponent of 1? For example, what is the value of 8^1?

_____

Reading Powers

7^2 "the 2nd power of 7" 7^3 "the 3rd power of 7"

7^4 "the 4th power of 7" 7^5 "the 5th power of 7" and so on...

2 **EXAMPLE** **Using Exponents to Write Expressions**

Use exponents to write each expression.

A $6 \times 6 \times 6 \times 6 \times 6 \times 6 \times 6$

What number is being multiplied? _____ This number is the base.

How many times does the base appear in the product? _____ This number is the exponent.

$6 \times 6 \times 6 \times 6 \times 6 \times 6 \times 6 =$ _____

B $\frac{2}{3} \times \frac{2}{3} \times \frac{2}{3}$

What number is being multiplied? _____ This number is the base.

How many times does the base appear in the product? _____ This number is the exponent.

$\frac{2}{3} \times \frac{2}{3} \times \frac{2}{3} =$ _____

TRY THIS!

Use exponents to write each expression.

2a. $3 \times 3 \times 3 \times 3 \times 3 \times 3 \times 3 \times 3$ _____   **2b.** $4 \times 4 \times 4$ _____

2c. 6 _____   **2d.** $\frac{1}{8} \times \frac{1}{8}$ _____   **2e.** $5 \times 5 \times 5 \times 5 \times 5 \times 5$ _____

3 **EXAMPLE** **Finding the Value of a Power**

Find the value of each power.

A 9^3

What is the base? _____

The exponent is 3, so the base will appear in the product 3 times.

$9^3 =$ _____ $\times$ _____ $\times$ _____ $=$ _____

B $\left(\frac{1}{2}\right)^2$

What is the base? _____ What is the exponent? _____

$\left(\frac{1}{2}\right)^2 = $ _____

TRY THIS!

Find the value of each power.

3a. 3^4 _____   **3b.** 1^9 _____   **3c.** $\left(\frac{2}{5}\right)^3$ _____   **3d.** 12^2 _____

4 **EXPLORE**   **Solving Problems Using Exponents**

Judah had two children. When those children grew up, each one also had two children, who later each had two children as well. If this pattern continues, how many children are there in the 7th generation?

You can use a diagram to model this situation. The first point at the top represents Judah. The other points represent children. Complete the diagram to show the 3rd generation.

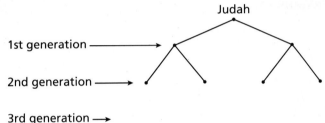

A How many children are in each generation?

1st _____   2nd _____   3rd _____

B Do you see a pattern in the numbers above? Try to find a pattern using exponents.

_____

C How is the number of children in a generation related to the generation number?

_____

D How many children will be in the 7th generation?

_____

TRY THIS!

4. A female guinea pig has about 4 litters per year, and a typical litter consists of 4 baby guinea pigs. How many baby guinea pigs would a typical female have in 4 years?

_____

Write each power.

1. the 10th power of 8 _____

2. the 8th power of 10 _____

3. the 11th power of $\frac{1}{2}$ _____

4. the 6th power of $\frac{2}{3}$ _____

Use exponents to write each expression.

5. $6 \times 6 \times 6$ _____

6. $10 \times 10 \times 10 \times 10 \times 10 \times 10 \times 10$ _____

7. $\frac{3}{4} \times \frac{3}{4} \times \frac{3}{4} \times \frac{3}{4} \times \frac{3}{4}$ _____

8. $\frac{7}{9} \times \frac{7}{9} \times \frac{7}{9} \times \frac{7}{9} \times \frac{7}{9} \times \frac{7}{9} \times \frac{7}{9} \times \frac{7}{9}$ _____

Find the value of each power.

9. 8^3 _____

10. 7^4 _____

11. 5^3 _____

12. 4^2 _____

13. $\left(\frac{1}{4}\right)^2$ _____

14. $\left(\frac{1}{3}\right)^3$ _____

15. $\left(\frac{6}{7}\right)^2$ _____

16. $\left(\frac{9}{10}\right)^1$ _____

Write the missing exponent.

17. $100 = 10^{\square}$

18. $8 = 2^{\square}$

19. $25 = 5^{\square}$

20. $27 = 3^{\square}$

21. $\frac{1}{169} = \left(\frac{1}{13}\right)^{\square}$

22. $14 = 14^{\square}$

23. $32 = 2^{\square}$

24. $\frac{64}{81} = \left(\frac{8}{9}\right)^{\square}$

Write the missing base.

25. $1,000 = \square^3$

26. $256 = \square^4$

27. $16 = \square^4$

28. $9 = \square^2$

29. $\frac{1}{9} = \left(\square\right)^2$

30. $64 = \square^2$

31. $\frac{9}{16} = \left(\square\right)^2$

32. $729 = \square^3$

33. Hadley's softball team has a phone tree in case a game is cancelled. The coach calls 3 players. Then each of those players calls 3 players, and so on. How many players will be notified during the 3rd round of calls? _____

34. Reasoning What is the value of all powers of 1? Explain.

_____

_____

3-2

Writing Expressions

Essential question: *How can you use variables and constants to write algebraic expressions?*

COMMON CORE

CC.6.EE.2a
CC.6.EE.6

1 EXPLORE   Using Variables to Describe Patterns

Look at the pattern of squares below.

Stage 1   Stage 2   Stage 3

A What is the pattern? _____

How many squares will be in stage 4? _____

B What is the relationship between the stage number and the number of squares?

_____

Use this relationship to complete the table below.

Stage	1	2	3	4	5	6	7	8
Squares	3	6	9					

C Let n represent any stage number. How many squares are in stage n?

_____

Add a column to the end of the table in **B** for stage n.

REFLECT

1. When might it be useful to know how many squares are in stage n?

_____

_____

_____

A **variable** is a letter or symbol used to represent an unknown or unspecified number. The value of a variable may change. In **1**, the variable n was used to represent any stage number.

A **constant** is a number that does not change. For example, the numbers 3, 8.6, and -21 are all constants because their values do not change.

An **algebraic expression** is an expression that contains one or more variables and may also contain operation symbols, such as $+$ or $-$.

Algebraic Expressions	$150 + y$ $w + n$ x
Not Algebraic Expressions	15 $12 - 7$ $\frac{9}{16}$

In algebraic expressions, multiplication and division are usually written without the symbols $\times$ and $\div$.

- Instead of $3 \times n$, write $3n$, $3 \cdot n$, or $n \cdot 3$.
- Instead of 3×5, write $3(5)$, $(3)5$, $(3)(5)$, or $3 \cdot 5$.
- Instead of $3 \div n$, write $\frac{3}{n}$.

Expressions can be written with constants and variables, or they may be described in words. When given an expression in words, it is important to be able to translate the words into algebra.

There are several different ways to describe expressions with words.

Operation	Addition	Subtraction	Multiplication	Division
Words	• added to • plus • sum • more than	• subtracted from • minus • difference • less than • take away • taken from	• times • multiplied by • product • groups of	• divided by • divided into • quotient

2 EXAMPLE Writing Algebraic Expressions

Write each phrase as an algebraic expression.

A **5 subtracted from _y_**

The operation is _____.

The algebraic expression is y ⬛ 5.

B **The product of 9 and _p_**

The operation is _____.

The algebraic expression is _____.

TRY THIS!

Write each phrase as an algebraic expression.

2a. _n_ times 7 _____
2b. 4 minus _y_ _____
2c. 13 added to _x_ _____

2d. _x_ divided by 9 _____
2e. 9 divided by _x_ _____
2f. _c_ plus 3 _____

2g. **Error Analysis** Erica wrote "5 added to y" as $5 + y$ and "5 subtracted from y" as $5 - y$. Why is the first expression correct but the second incorrect? When is order important in writing an expression?

_____

_____

_____

When solving real-world problems, you may need to identify the action taking place to know which operation to use.

Action	Operation
Put parts together	Addition
Put equal parts together	Multiplication
Find how much more or less	Subtraction
Separate into equal parts	Division

3 EXAMPLE Translating Words into Algebraic Expressions

Center City is 10 miles farther from Sam's house than Westonville is. Write an algebraic expression to represent the distance from Sam's house to Center City.

Let w represent the distance from Sam's house to Westonville.

The distance from Sam's house to Center City is 10 miles more / less than w.

So, to find the distance from Sam's house to Center City, put together
_____ and _____.

Which operation represents this action? _____

The distance from Sam's house to Center City can be represented by the
expression _____.

TRY THIS!

3a. Sonia worked 25 hours last week. She was paid the same amount of money per hour that she worked. Let h represent Sonia's hourly pay. Write an algebraic expression that represents Sonia's total pay last week.

_____

3b. Noah is saving to buy a new laptop computer. He has saved $119 so far. Let c represent the cost of the laptop. Write an algebraic expression that represents the amount of money Noah still needs to save.

_____

1. Identify the constant(s) and variable(s) in the algebraic expression $t - 4n + 2$.

   Constant(s) _____   Variable(s) _____

2. Circle the algebraic expression(s) in the list below.

   $180 + 25$ $x - 79$ $7(12)$ $a + b$ -220 $13t$ $\frac{n}{16}$ $24 - 3h$ $\frac{4}{7}$ r

Write each phrase as an algebraic expression.

3. n divided by 8 _____

4. p multiplied by 4 _____

5. b plus 14 _____

6. 90 times x _____

7. a take away 16 _____

8. k less than 24 _____

9. 3 groups of w _____

10. the sum of 1 and q _____

11. the quotient of 13 and z _____

12. c added to 45 _____

Write a phrase in words for each algebraic expression.

13. $m + 83$ _____

14. $42s$ _____

15. $\frac{9}{d}$ _____

16. $t - 29$ _____

17. $2 + g$ _____

18. $11x$ _____

19. $\frac{h}{12}$ _____

20. $5 - k$ _____

21. Kayla's score on yesterday's math test was 12 points greater than Julianne's score. Let k represent Kayla's score. Write an algebraic expression to represent Julianne's score.

   _____

22. The town of Rayburn received 6 more inches of snow than the town of Greenville. Let g represent the amount of snow in Greenville. Write an algebraic expression to represent the amount of snow in Rayburn.

   _____

23. Abby baked 48 cookies and divided them evenly into bags. Let b represent the number of bags. Write an algebraic expression to represent the number of cookies in each bag.

   _____

24. Eli is driving at a speed of 55 miles per hour. Let h represent the number of hours that Eli drives at this speed. Write an algebraic expression to represent the number of miles that Eli travels during this time.

   _____

Parts of an Expression

Essential question: *How do you identify and describe parts of an expression?*

1 EXPLORE Definitions

A Write the definitions of these words from Lesson 3-2 in your own words.

variable _____

_____

constant _____

_____

algebraic expression _____

_____

B In the expressions 9*a*, 5*y*, 6*n*, and 12*x*, the blue numbers are *coefficients*.
Write a definition of *coefficient* in your own words.

coefficient _____

_____

C The expression 5*y* + *z* − 8 has three terms. The expression 15 + *x* has two terms.
The expression 5*c* has one term. Write a definition of *term* in your own words.

term _____

_____

D Compare your definitions in **B** and **C** to those of other students and discuss
any differences in them. If necessary, make changes to your definitions.

E Use words from the box to complete each sentence.

factor	product	quotient	sum	difference

15 + *x* represents a _____ of two terms.

9*a* represents the _____ of 9 and *a*.

p ÷ 3 represents a _____ .

12 − *x* is a _____ of two terms.

1. **Conjecture** What is the coefficient of a term that consists of a single variable? For example, what is the coefficient of x? _____

2 EXPLORE Describing Expressions

There may be several different ways to describe a given expression.

A Write each description on individual index cards or sticky notes.

algebraic expression	sum of two terms	product of two factors	sum of a quotient and a constant	product of a coefficient and a variable

B Write each of the following expressions at the top of its own sheet of paper. Then place the index card(s) or sticky note(s) that describe an expression onto its paper. Write the descriptions you placed on each paper next to the expression.

$\frac{9a}{5} + 32$ _____

_____

$3(m + 1)$ _____

_____

$7c$ _____

_____

$5 + 9$ _____

_____

C Compare your answers in **B** with those of other students and make changes to them, if necessary.

TRY THIS!

Write an algebraic expression that matches each description.

2a. A product of two variables _____

2b. A sum of a product and a constant _____

2c. An expression with 3 terms _____

2d. A product of two factors, where one factor is a difference of two terms

_____

Evaluating Expressions

COMMON
CORE

CC.6.EE.2c

Essential question: *How do you evaluate expressions?*

Recall that an algebraic expression contains one or more variables. You can substitute a number for that variable and then find the value of the expression. This is called **evaluating** the expression.

1 EXAMPLE Evaluating Expressions

Evaluate each expression for the given value of the variable.

A $x - 9; x = 15$

$\boxed{} - 9$ *Substitute 15 for x.*

$\boxed{}$ *Subtract.*

When $x = 15$, $x - 9 = \boxed{}$.

B $n + 19; n = 8$

$\boxed{} + 19$ *Substitute 8 for n.*

$\boxed{}$ *Add.*

When $n = 8$, $n + 19 = \boxed{}$.

C $0.5y; y = 1.4$

$0.5\left(\boxed{}\right)$ *Substitute 1.4 for y.*

$\boxed{}$ *Multiply.*

When $y = 1.4$, $0.5y = \boxed{}$.

D $6k; k = \frac{1}{3}$

$6\left(\dfrac{\boxed{}}{\boxed{}}\right)$ *Substitute $\frac{1}{3}$ for k.*

$\boxed{}$ *Multiply.*

When $k = \frac{1}{3}$, $6k = \boxed{}$.

TRY THIS!

Evaluate each expression for the given value of the variable.

1a. $4x; x = 8$ _____   **1b.** $6.5 - n; n = 1.8$ _____   **1c.** $\frac{m}{6}; m = 18$ _____

To evaluate expressions with more than one operation, use the order of operations.

> ## Order of Operations
> 1. Perform operations in parentheses.
> 2. Find the values of numbers with exponents.
> 3. Multiply or divide from left to right as ordered in the expression.
> 4. Add or subtract from left to right as ordered in the expression.

2 EXAMPLE Using the Order of Operations

Evaluate each expression for $x = 7$.

A $4(x - 4)$

$4\left(\boxed{} - 4\right)$ — *Substitute 7 for x.*

$4\left(\boxed{}\right)$ — *Subtract inside the parentheses.*

$\boxed{}$ — *Multiply.*

B $4x - 4$

$4\left(\boxed{}\right) - 4$ — *Substitute 7 for x.*

$\boxed{} - 4$ — *Multiply.*

$\boxed{}$ — *Subtract.*

C $x^2 + x$

$\left(\boxed{}\right)^2 + \boxed{}$ — *Substitute 7 for x.*

$\boxed{} + 7$ — *Find the values of numbers with exponents.*

$\boxed{}$ — *Add.*

REFLECT

2a. The answers to **A** and **B** are not the same, even though the expressions are very similar. Why?

_____

_____

TRY THIS!

Evaluate each expression for $n = 5$.

2b. $3(n + 1)$ _____

2c. $3n + 1$ _____

2d. $(4n - 4) + 14$ _____

2e. $4n - (4 + 14)$ _____

2f. $4(n - 4) + 14$ _____

2g. $6n + n^2$ _____

3 EXAMPLE **Expressions with More than One Variable**

Evaluate $w - x + y$ for $w = 6$, $x = 5$, and $y = 3$.

[ ] − [ ] + [ ]   *Substitute* [ ] *for w,* [ ] *for x, and* [ ] *for y.*

[ ] + 3   *Subtract.*

[ ]   *Add.*

REFLECT

3a. In this example, why do you subtract before adding?

_____

_____

TRY THIS!

Evaluate each expression for $a = 3$, $b = 4$, and $c = 5$.

3b. $ab - c$ _____   **3c.** $bc + 5a$ _____

4 EXAMPLE **Using Formulas**

The expression $2(\ell w + \ell h + hw)$ gives the surface area of a rectangular prism with length ℓ, width w, and height h. Find the surface area of the rectangular prism shown.

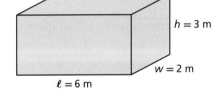
$h = 3$ m
$w = 2$ m
$\ell = 6$ m

Use the diagram to find the values of ℓ, w, and h.

$\ell =$ [ ] $w =$ [ ] $h =$ [ ]

Substitute these values into the expression $2(\ell w + \ell h + hw)$.

$2\left[\left(\ \right)\left(\ \right) + \left(\ \right)\left(\ \right) + \left(\ \right)\left(\ \right)\right]$

$= 2\left(\ [\ ] + [\ ] + [\ ]\ \right)$ *Multiply inside the parentheses.*

$= 2\left(\ [\ ]\ \right)$ *Add inside the parentheses.*

$= [\ ]$ *Multiply.*

The surface area of the rectangular prism is [ ] m^2.

TRY THIS!

4a. The expression $6x^2$ gives the surface area of a cube, and the expression x^3 gives the volume of a cube, where x is the length of one side of the cube. Find the surface area and the volume of a cube with a side length of 2 m.
$S =$ _____ m^2; $V =$ _____ m^3

4b. The expression $60m$ gives the number of seconds in m minutes. How many seconds are there in 7 minutes? _____ seconds

PRACTICE

Evaluate each expression for the given value(s) of the variable(s).

1. $x - 7$; $x = 23$ _____

2. $3r$; $r = 6$ _____

3. $\frac{8}{t}$; $t = 4$ _____

4. $9 + m$; $m = 1.5$ _____

5. $p - 2$; $p = 19$ _____

6. $3h$; $h = \frac{1}{6}$ _____

7. $2.5 - n$; $n = 1.8$ _____

8. k^2; $k = 4$ _____

9. $4(b - 4)$; $b = 5$ _____

10. $38 - \frac{x}{2}$; $x = 12$ _____

11. $\frac{30}{d} - 2$; $d = 6$ _____

12. $x^2 - 34$; $x = 10$ _____

13. $\frac{1}{2}w + 2$; $w = \frac{1}{9}$ _____

14. $5(6.2 + z)$; $z = 3.8$ _____

15. $2a^2 + a$; $a = 8$ _____

16. $7y + 32$; $y = 9$ _____

17. xy; $x = 8$ and $y = 6$

_____

18. $x + y - 1$; $x = 12$ and $y = 4$

_____

19. $3x + 4y$; $x = 4$ and $y = 5$

_____

20. $4x + 1 + 3y$; $x = 6$ and $y = 8$

_____

21. The expression ℓwh gives the volume of a rectangular prism with length ℓ, width w, and height h. Find the volume of the rectangular prism. _____ in^3

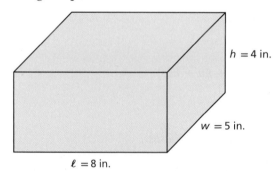

$h = 4$ in.

$w = 5$ in.

$\ell = 8$ in.

22. The expression $1.8c + 32$ gives the temperature in degrees Fahrenheit for a given temperature in degrees Celsius c. Find the temperature in degrees Fahrenheit that is equivalent to 30 °C. _____°F

23. Error Analysis Marjorie evaluated the expression $3x + 2$ for $x = 5$ as shown:

$$3x + 2 = 35 + 2 = 37$$

What was Marjorie's mistake? What is the correct value of $3x + 2$ for $x = 5$?

_____

Equivalent Expressions

COMMON CORE

CC.6.EE.3
CC.6.EE.4

Essential question: *How can you identify and write equivalent expressions?*

Equivalent expressions are expressions that simplify to the same value for any numbers(s) substituted for the variable(s). For example, the expression $y + y + y$ is equivalent to $3y$ because the two expressions will have the same value for any number that is substituted for y.

1 EXPLORE Identifying Equivalent Expressions

Match the expressions in List A with their equivalent expressions in List B.

List A	List B
$5x + 65$	$5x + 1$
$5(x + 1)$	$5x + 5$
$1 + 5x$	$5(13 + x)$

A One way to test whether two expressions might be equivalent is to evaluate them for the same value of the variable. Evaluate each of the expressions in the lists for $x = 3$.

List A	List B
$5(3) + 65 = \boxed{}$	$5(3) + 1 = \boxed{}$
$5(3 + 1) = \boxed{}$	$5(3) + 5 = \boxed{}$
$1 + 5(3) = \boxed{}$	$5(13 + 3) = \boxed{}$

B Which pair(s) of expressions have the same value for $x = 3$?

_____

C How could you further test whether the expressions in each pair are equivalent?

_____

_____

D Do you think the expressions in each pair are equivalent? Why or why not?

_____

_____

1a. Lisa evaluated the expressions $2x$ and x^2 for $x = 2$ and found that both expressions were equal to 4. Lisa concluded that $2x$ and x^2 are equivalent expressions. How could you show Lisa that she is incorrect?

_____

_____

1b. What does **1a** demonstrate about expressions?

_____

_____

Properties of operations can be used to identify equivalent expressions.

Properties of Operations	Examples
Commutative Property of Addition: When adding, changing the order of the numbers does not change the sum.	$3 + 4 = 4 + 3$
Commutative Property of Multiplication: When multiplying, changing the order of the numbers does not change the product.	$2 \times 4 = 4 \times 2$
Associative Property of Addition: When adding more than two numbers, the grouping of the numbers does not change the sum.	$(3 + 4) + 5 = 3 + (4 + 5)$
Associative Property of Multiplication: When multiplying more than two numbers, the grouping of the numbers does not change the product.	$(2 \times 4) \times 3 = 2 \times (4 \times 3)$
Distributive Property: Multiplying a number by a sum or difference is the same as multiplying by each number in the sum or difference and then adding or subtracting.	$6(2 + 4) = 6(2) + 6(4)$ $8(5 - 3) = 8(5) - 8(3)$

2 EXAMPLE Writing Equivalent Expressions

Use one of the properties in the table above to write an expression that is equivalent to $x + 3$.

The operation in the expression is _____.

Which property of this operation can be applied to $x + 3$?

_____

Use this property to write an equivalent expression:

$x + 3 =$ _____

For each expression, use a property to write an equivalent expression. Tell which property you used.

2a. $(ab)c = $ _____

2b. $3y + 4y = $ _____

Recall that terms are the parts of an expression that are added or subtracted. A term may contain variables, constants, or both. **Like terms** are terms with the same variable(s) raised to the same power(s). All constants are like terms.

$12 + 3y^3 + 4x + 2y^3$ $3y^3$ and $2y^3$ are like terms.

$5 + 8x + 13$ 5 and 13 are like terms.

3 EXAMPLE   Identifying Like Terms

Identify the like terms in the list.

$5a$ $3y^3$ $7t$ x^2 $4x$ y $2y^3$ $2t$ $2a$ $2a^2$

First, identify the terms that have the same variable.

Terms with a: _____   Terms with t: _____

Terms with x: _____   Terms with y: _____

Within each list above, circle the terms that have the same exponent.

The like terms are _____ and _____; _____ and _____; _____ and _____.

REFLECT

3.   The terms y and $2y^3$ contain the same variable but are not like terms. Why not? _____

When an expression contains like terms, you can use properties to combine the like terms into a single term. This results in an expression that is equivalent to the original expression.

4 EXAMPLE   Combining Like Terms

Combine like terms.

A $6x^2 - 4x^2$

   $6x^2$ and $4x^2$ are like terms.

   $6x^2 - 4x^2 = x^2(6 - 4)$ *Distributive Property*

   $ = x^2\left(\boxed{}\right)$ *Subtract inside the parentheses.*

   $ = \boxed{}\, x^2$ *Commutative Property of Multiplication*

   $6x^2 - 4x^2 = $ _____

B $3a + 2(b + 5a)$

$$3a + 2(b + 5a) = 3a + 2b + 2(5a)$$ *Distributive Property*

$$= 3a + 2b + (2 \cdot 5)a$$ *Associative Property of Multiplication*

$$= 3a + 2b + \boxed{}\, a$$ *Multiply 2 and 5.*

$$= 3a + 10a + 2b$$ _____ *Property of Addition*

$$= (3 + 10)a + 2b$$ *Distributive Property*

$$= \boxed{}\, a + 2b$$ *Add inside the parentheses.*

$$3a + 2(b + 5a) = \underline{\hspace{3cm}}$$

TRY THIS!

Combine like terms.

4a. $8y - 3y =$ _____

4b. $6x^2 + 4(x^2 - 1) =$ _____

4c. $4a^5 - 2a^5 + 4b + b =$ _____

4d. $8m + 14 - 12 + 4n =$ _____

PRACTICE

1. Draw lines to match the expressions in List A with their equivalent expressions in List B.

<u>List A</u>	<u>List B</u>
$4 + 4b$	$4b - 4$
$4(b - 1)$	$4(b + 1)$
$4b + 1$	$1 + 4b$

For each expression, use a property to write an equivalent expression. Tell which property you used.

2. $ab =$ _____

3. $x + 13 =$ _____

4. $5(3x - 2) =$ _____

5. $2 + (a + b) =$ _____

Circle the like terms in each list.

6. $3a$ $16a$ 5 y $2a^2$

7. $5x^3$ $3y$ $7x^3$ $4x$ 21

8. $6b^2$ $2a^2$ $4a^3$ b^2 b

9. $12t^2$ $4x^3$ a $4t^2$ 1 $2t^2$

10. $32y$ 5 $3y^2$ 17 y^3 6

11. $10k^2$ m 9 $2m$ $10k$

Combine like terms.

12. $7x^4 - 5x^4 =$ _____

13. $2x + 3x + 4 =$ _____

14. $6b + 7b - 10 =$ _____

15. $32y + 5y =$ _____

16. $y + 4 + 3(y + 2) =$ _____

17. $7a^2 - a^2 + 16 =$ _____

Problem Solving Connections

How Much Paint? Jody's family has moved into a new house, and Jody is going to repaint her new bedroom. Jody's dad says that she first has to calculate how much paint to buy. How can Jody use algebraic expressions to find the amount of paint she will need?

COMMON CORE

CC.6.EE.1
CC.6.EE.2a, b, c
CC.6.EE.3
CC.6.EE.4
CC.6.EE.6

1 Write Expressions

A Jody's bedroom is rectangular. Let a represent the width (shorter side) of the room, and let b represent the length (longer side). Let c represent the height of each wall.

The rectangular prism below can be used to model Jody's bedroom. Label a, b, and c on the prism.

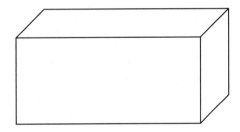

B Write an algebraic expression to represent the combined area of the two larger walls of the room. Explain your thinking.

_____

_____

C Write an algebraic expression to represent the combined area of the two smaller walls. Explain your thinking.

_____

_____

D Write an algebraic expression to represent the area of the ceiling.

_____

E Use your answers above to write an algebraic expression to represent the total area of all four walls and the ceiling.

_____

2 Evaluate Expressions

A Now Jody must measure her bedroom so she can substitute the measurements into the algebraic expressions. First Jody measures the height c of the walls and the length b of the longer wall. She finds that $c = 12$ feet and $b = 20$ feet.

Rewrite the expression that represents the combined area of the two larger walls. Then evaluate this expression using the values of b and c that Jody found. What is the total area of these two walls?

B Jody cannot reach high enough to measure the ceiling, so she measures the floor instead. She already knows that the longer side of the floor b measures 20 feet. She finds that the shorter side a measures 8 feet.

Rewrite the expression that represents the area of the ceiling. Then evaluate this expression using the values of a and b that Jody found. What is the area of the ceiling?

C Does Jody need to measure anything else to find the area of the two smaller walls? Why or why not?

_____

_____

D Rewrite the expression that represents the combined area of the two smaller walls. Then evaluate this expression using the appropriate values. What is the total area of these two walls?

E Find the total area of the four walls and the ceiling. Explain how you found your answer.

F "Now we can go to the paint store and buy the paint," Jody says. "Wait!" says Dad. "Some of the walls are not really rectangles. Your room has a door and two square windows. You can paint the door if you want, but you are definitely not going to paint the windows!" After thinking about it, Jody decides that she will paint her door.

Both windows are the same size. Let s represent the side length of one of the windows. Write an algebraic expression with an exponent to represent the combined area of both windows. Explain your thinking.

G Jody returns to her room to measure one of the windows. She measures the window's length as 4 feet.

Rewrite the expression that represents the combined area of the two windows. Then evaluate that expression using Jody's measurement. What is the total area of the two windows?

H Explain how you used the order of operations to evaluate the expression for the windows' area.

I What operation should Jody use to find the total area of the surfaces she is going to paint?

Find the total area that Jody will paint.

3 Answer the Question

A   Jody and her dad arrive at the paint store, where Jody chooses two paint colors—light blue for the walls and white for the ceiling.

Look back to find the area of the ceiling and write it here: _____ ft^2

How can Jody find the total area of just the four walls (not including the ceiling)?

_____

Find the area of only the four walls.

B   The label on each paint can reads "Covers 300 square feet." Jody reasons that the area of the four walls is about 600 ft^2, so she will need $\frac{600}{300} = 2$ cans of blue paint. Do you agree with Jody? Why or why not? If not, how many cans of blue paint do you think Jody should buy?

_____

_____

C   How many cans of white paint does Jody need? Explain your thinking.

_____

_____

D   The paint store associate recommends that Jody put two coats on each surface to completely cover the existing color. Does one can of white paint contain enough paint for two coats on the ceiling? Explain.

_____

_____

Jody and her dad agree with the paint store associate and decide to apply two coats. Jody says, "Then we need twice as much paint, two cans of white paint and six cans of blue paint." Is Jody correct? Explain.

_____

_____

_____

_____

Name _____ **Class** _____ **Date** _____

MULTIPLE CHOICE

1. Which is a shorthand way to write
$5 \times 5 \times 5 \times 5$?

A. $5 \times 5 + 5 \times 5$ **C.** 5^4

B. 5^3 **D.** 4^5

2. Which word describes a number that tells
you how many times to multiply a number
by itself?

F. Variable   **H.** Expression

G. Exponent   **J.** Constant

3. Andre made the table below to show
the results of his experiments on the
reproduction of flies.

Day	Number of Flies	Total
1	3	3
2	3×3	9
3	$3 \times 3 \times 3$	27
4	$3 \times 3 \times 3 \times 3$	81

How could Andre write his results for
day 4 using exponents?

A. 4^2 **C.** 3^2

B. 3^3 **D.** 3^4

4. Erik made a model train that was 25 feet
shorter in length than an actual train. Let
m represent the length of Erik's model.
Which expression represents the length of
the actual train?

F. $25 - m$ **H.** $m + 25$

G. $25m$ **J.** $m - 25$

5. Which of the following expressions is
equivalent to $7x + 12$?

A. $12 + 7x$ **C.** $19x$

B. $7 + 12x$ **D.** $7(x + 12)$

6. Mark has been asked to find the value of
$4(9 + 24) + 7$. What should he do first?

F. Add 4 and 7.

G. Multiply 4 and 9.

H. Multiply 4 and 24.

J. Add 9 and 24.

7. The new county park has an area that
is 3.5 times the area of the old park. Let
p represent the area of the old park.
Which expression represents the area of
the new park?

A. $3.5p$ **C.** $p + 3.5$

B. $p - 3.5$ **D.** $\frac{p}{3.5}$

8. Which of the following is an example
of the Commutative Property
of Multiplication?

F. $(15 \times 5) \times 5 = 15 \times (5 \times 5)$

G. $15 \times 5 = 5 \times 15$

H. $5 + 15 = 15 + 5$

J. $5(15 + 5) = 5(5 + 15)$

9. Evaluate the expression $24x - 13y$ for
$x = 3$ and $y = 2$.

A. 11   **C.** 37

B. 33   **D.** 46

10. Which expression does **not** equal 15?

F. $3k$ for $k = 5$

G. $3 + k$ for $k = 12$

H. $\frac{k}{3}$ for $k = 60$

J. $k - 10$ for $k = 25$

11. Combine like terms in $5m^2 + 16k^2 + 13m^2$.

A. $34m^2$ **C.** $18m^2 + 16k^2$

B. $34k^2$ **D.** $18m^4 + 16k^2$

12. The new building in City Center is 345 feet taller than the Jefferson Building. Let h represent the height of the Jefferson Building. Which expression represents the height of the new building?

F. $h + 345$ H. $h - 345$

G. $345 - h$ J. $345h$

13. $5(20 + x) = 5(20) + 5x$ is an example of which property?

A. Associative Property of Addition

B. Associative Property of Multiplication

C. Commutative Property of Addition

D. Distributive Property

14. Which expression contains like terms?

F. $x + y + xy$ H. $7y^2 - 7y - 7$

G. $17x^2 + x^3 + x$ J. $x^4 + 15 + 4x^4$

15. Which expression is equivalent to $9n + 3$ after combining like terms?

A. $10n^2 - n^2 - 3$

B. $3n + 7 - 4 + 3n$

C. $18 - 15 + 4n + 5n$

D. $7n^2 + 2n + 6 - 3$

16. Which expression has a value of 74 when $a = 10$, $b = 8$, and $c = 12$?

F. $4abc$ H. $2ac - 3b$

G. $a + 5b + 2c$ J. $6abc + 8$

17. Which quantity **cannot** be represented by the expression $0.20x$?

A. The total cost of x text messages, where each text message costs $0.20

B. The total amount of calcium in x servings of a cereal that contains 0.2 gram of calcium per serving

C. The area of a rectangle with length x and width 0.2

D. The amount of change due when an item that costs $0.20 is paid for with x dollars

FREE RESPONSE

18. Write two different phrases in words that describe the expression $7z$.

_____

_____

19. Write an algebraic expression...

a. that has three terms. _____

b. in which one term is the product of two variables. _____

c. that is the sum of a product and a constant. _____

20. The distance from Ray's house to the shopping center is 3.5 miles more then the distance from Ray's house to the city park.

a. Let c equal the distance from Ray's house to the city park. Write an expression to represent the distance from Ray's house to the shopping center.

_____

b. The distance from Ray's house to the city park is 2 miles. How can you use this information and your answer to part **a** to find the distance from Ray's house to the shopping center?

_____

c. What is the distance from Ray's house to the shopping center?

_____

21. a. What is the first step in finding the value of $12 + (6 + 4)$?

_____

b. $12 + (6 + 4) =$ _____

c. What is the first step in finding the value of $(12 + 6) + 4$?

_____

d. $(12 + 6) + 4 =$ _____

e. What property is demonstrated by your answers to parts **b** and **d**?

_____

Equations

Unit Focus

You have already learned how to write and evaluate expressions and to identify parts of an expression. In this unit, you will learn to solve equations and use substitution to check solutions. You will analyze relationships between variables using equations, tables, and graphs. You will also learn about inequalities.

Unit at a Glance

COMMON
CORE

Lesson		Standards for Mathematical Content
4-1	Equations and Solutions	CC.6.EE.5, CC.6.EE.6
4-2	Addition and Subtraction Equations	CC.6.EE.7
4-3	Multiplication and Division Equations	CC.6.EE.7
4-4	Equations, Tables, and Graphs	CC.6.EE.9
4-5	Solutions of Inequalities	CC.6.EE.5, CC.6.EE.6, CC.6.EE.8
	Problem Solving Connections	
	Test Prep	

Unpacking the Common Core Standards

Use the table to help you understand the Standards for Mathematical Content that are taught in this unit. Refer to the lessons listed after each standard for exploration and practice.

COMMON CORE Standards for Mathematical Content	What It Means For You
CC.6.EE.5 Understand solving an equation or inequality as a process of answering a question: which values from a specified set, if any, make the equation or inequality true? Use substitution to determine whether a given number in a specified set makes an equation or inequality true. Lessons 4-1, 4-5	You will learn how to use substitution to determine whether a number is a solution of an equation or inequality.
CC.6.EE.6 Use variables to represent numbers and write expressions when solving a real-world or mathematical problem; understand that a variable can represent an unknown number, or, depending on the purpose at hand, any number in a specified set. Lessons 4-1, 4-5	You will write expressions to represent real-world or mathematical problems.
CC.6.EE.7 Solve real-world and mathematical problems by writing and solving equations of the form $x + p = q$ and $px = q$ for cases in which p, q and x are all nonnegative rational numbers. Lessons 4-2, 4-3	You will use your knowledge of operations to solve equations.
CC.6.EE.8 Write an inequality of the form $x > c$ or $x < c$ to represent a constraint or condition in a real-world or mathematical problem. Recognize that inequalities of the form $x > c$ or $x < c$ have infinitely many solutions; represent solutions of such inequalities on number line diagrams. Lesson 4-5	You will understand that an inequality has many solutions and you will graph these solutions on a number line. You will write inequalities to represent real-world situations.
CC.6.EE.9 Use variables to represent two quantities in a real-world problem that change in relationship to one another; write an equation to express one quantity, thought of as the dependent variable, in terms of the other quantity, thought of as the independent variable. Analyze the relationship between the dependent and independent variables using graphs and tables, and relate these to the equation. Lesson 4-4	You will analyze relationships between two variables and write equations in two variables to represent real-world problems.

Equations and Solutions

Essential question: *How do you determine whether a number is a solution of an equation?*

COMMON CORE

CC.6.EE.5
CC.6.EE.6

An **equation** is a mathematical statement that two expressions are equal. An equation may or may not contain variables. For an equation that has a variable, a **solution** of the equation is a value of the variable that makes the equation true.

1 EXAMPLE **Checking Solutions**

Determine whether the given value is a solution of the equation.

A $x + 9 = 15; x = 6$

$\boxed{} + 9 \stackrel{?}{=} 15$ *Substitute 6 for x.*

$\boxed{} \stackrel{?}{=} 15$ *Add.*

6 is / is not a solution of $x + 9 = 15$.

B $5 = t - 4; t = 11$

$5 \stackrel{?}{=} \boxed{} - 4$ *Substitute 11 for t.*

$5 \stackrel{?}{=} \boxed{}$ *Subtract.*

11 is / is not a solution of $5 = t - 4$.

C $8x = 72; x = 9$

$8 \left(\boxed{} \right) \stackrel{?}{=} 72$ *Substitute 9 for x.*

$\boxed{} \stackrel{?}{=} 72$ *Multiply.*

9 is / is not a solution of $8x = 72$.

D $\frac{y}{4} = 32; y = 8$

$\dfrac{\boxed{}}{4} \stackrel{?}{=} 32$ *Substitute 8 for y.*

$\boxed{} \stackrel{?}{=} 32$ *Divide.*

8 is / is not a solution of $\frac{y}{4} = 32$.

Determine whether the given value is a solution of the equation.

1a. $11 = n + 6; n = 5$ **1b.** $y - 6 = 24; y = 18$ **1c.** $\frac{36}{x} = 9; x = 4$

_____   _____   _____

REFLECT

1d. Write an equation containing a variable that has a solution of 16.

_____

2 EXAMPLE   Writing an Equation

Mark scored 17 points in a basketball game. His teammates scored a total of _p_ points, and the team as a whole scored 46 points. Write an equation to represent this situation.

Mark's points	+	Teammates' points	=	Total points

$$\square \quad + \quad \square \quad = \quad \square$$

REFLECT

2a. Write an equation containing an operation other than addition that also represents the situation.

_____

TRY THIS!

Write an equation to represent each situation.

2b. Marilyn has a fish tank that contains 38 fish. There are 9 goldfish and f other fish.

_____

2c. Juanita has 102 beads to make n necklaces. Each necklace will have 17 beads.

_____

2d. Craig is c years old. His 12-year-old sister Caitlin is 3 years younger than Craig.

_____

2e. Sonia rented ice skates for h hours. The rental fee was \$2 per hour and she paid a total of \$8.

_____

Sarah used a gift card to buy $47 worth of groceries. Now she has $18 left on her gift card. Write an equation to determine whether Sarah had $65 or $59 on the gift card before buying groceries.

A The boxes below represent the three quantities given in the problem. Write an equation to show the relationship between these quantities by writing mathematical symbols between the boxes.

Amount on card		Amount spent		Amount left on card

Which two quantities in the equation are known?

_____

Rewrite the equation, substituting numbers from the problem for the two known quantities. Substitute the variable x for the unknown quantity.

_____

B How can you use the equation from **A** to check whether Sarah had $65 or $59 on the gift card before buying groceries?

_____

Use the space below to check whether Sarah had $65 or $59 before buying groceries.

The amount on Sarah's gift card before she bought groceries was $_____.

TRY THIS!

3a. Pedro bought 8 tickets to a basketball game. He paid a total of $208. Write an equation to determine whether each ticket cost $26 or $28.

_____

3b. On Saturday morning, Owen earned $24 raking leaves. By the end of the afternoon he had earned a total of $62. Write an equation to determine whether Owen earned $38 or $31 on Saturday afternoon.

_____

Determine whether the given value is a solution of the equation.

1. $23 = x - 9; x = 14$ _____

2. $\frac{n}{13} = 4; n = 52$ _____

3. $14 + x = 46; x = 32$ _____

4. $17y = 85; y = 5$ _____

5. $25 = \frac{k}{5}; k = 5$ _____

6. $2.5n = 45; n = 18$ _____

7. $21 = m + 9; m = 11$ _____

8. $21 - h = 15; h = 6$ _____

9. $d - 4 = 19; d = 15$ _____

10. $5 + x = 47; x = 52$ _____

11. $w - 9 = 0; w = 9$ _____

12. $5q = 31; q = 13$ _____

13. $7a = 126; a = 18$ _____

14. $3.6 = 3c; c = 1.2$ _____

15. $\frac{1}{2}r = 8; r = 4$ _____

16. $9x = 117; x = 12$ _____

For 17–19, write an equation to represent the situation.

17. Each floor of a hotel has r rooms. On 8 floors, there are a total of 256 rooms.

_____

18. Mario had b books. After receiving 5 new books for his birthday, he had 18 books.

_____

19. In the school band, there are 5 trumpet players and f flute players. There are twice as many flute players as there are trumpet players.

_____

20. Halfway through a bus route, 48 students remain on the bus, and 23 students have already been dropped off. Write an equation to determine whether there are 61 or 71 students on the bus at the beginning of the route.

_____

21. The high temperature was 92 °F. This was 24 °F higher than the overnight low temperature. Write an equation to determine whether the low temperature was 62 °F or 68 °F.

_____

22. Andy is one-fourth as old as his grandfather, who is 76 years old. Write an equation to determine whether Andy is 19 or 22 years old.

_____

Addition and Subtraction Equations

COMMON CORE

CC.6.EE.7

Essential question: *How do you solve equations that contain addition or subtraction?*

1 **EXPLORE** **Addition Equations**

A puppy weighed 6 ounces at birth. After two weeks, the puppy weighed 14 ounces. How much weight did the puppy gain?

Let x represent the number of ounces gained.

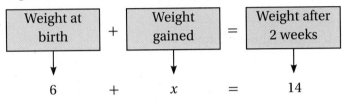

| Weight at birth | + | Weight gained | = | Weight after 2 weeks |

$$6 \quad + \quad x \quad = \quad 14$$

To answer this question, you can solve the equation $6 + x = 14$.

Algebra tiles can model some equations. An equation mat represents the two sides of an equation. To solve the equation, remove the same number of tiles from both sides of the mat until the x-tile is by itself on one side.

A Model $6 + x = 14$.

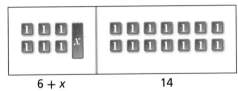

$6 + x$ 14

B How many unit tiles must you remove on the left side so that the x-tile is by itself? _____ Cross out these tiles on the equation mat.

C Whenever you remove tiles from one side of the mat, you must remove the same number of tiles from the other side of the mat. Cross out the tiles that should be removed on the right side of the mat.

D How many tiles remain on the right side of the mat? _____ This is the solution of the equation.

The puppy gained _____ ounces.

TRY THIS!

Solve each equation.

1a. $x + 2 = 7$

$x =$ _____

1b. $x + 9 = 12$

$x =$ _____

1c. $6 + x = 11$

$x =$ _____

Removing the same number of tiles from each side of an equation mat models subtracting the same number from both sides of an equation.

> **Subtraction Property of Equality**
>
> You can subtract the same number from both sides of an equation, and the two sides will remain equal.

When an equation contains addition, solve by subtracting the same number from both sides.

2 EXAMPLE Using the Subtraction Property of Equality

Solve each equation.

A $a + 15 = 26$

What number is added to a? _____

Subtract this number from both sides of the equation.

$$a + \quad 15 \quad = \quad 26$$

$$-\boxed{} \quad -\boxed{}$$

_____   _____

$$a \qquad = \boxed{} \qquad \textit{Subtract.}$$

Check: $a + 15 = 26$

$$\boxed{} + 15 \overset{?}{=} 26 \qquad \textit{Substitute } \boxed{} \textit{ for a.}$$

$$\boxed{} \overset{?}{=} 26 \qquad \textit{Add on the left side.}$$

B $23 = d + 17$

What number is added to d? _____

Subtract this number from both sides of the equation.

$$23 \quad = d \ + \ 17$$

$$-\boxed{} \qquad -\boxed{}$$

_____   _____

$$\boxed{} = d \qquad \textit{Subtract.}$$

TRY THIS!

Solve each equation.

2a. $n + 34 = 56$ **2b.** $w + 31 = 72$ **2c.** $z - 7.12 = 0.54$

$n =$ _____ $w =$ _____ $z =$ _____

When an equation contains subtraction, solve by adding the same number to both sides.

> **Addition Property of Equality**
>
> You can add the same number to both sides of an equation, and the two sides will remain equal.

3 EXAMPLE Using the Addition Property of Equality

Solve each equation.

A $y - 21 = 18$

What number is subtracted from y? _____

Add this number to both sides of the equation.

$$y - \quad 21 = \quad 18$$
$$+ \boxed{} = + \boxed{}$$
$$\overline{} \quad \overline{}$$
$$y \qquad = \boxed{} \qquad Add.$$

B $31 = g - 16$

What number is subtracted from g? _____

Add this number to both sides of the equation.

$$31 = g - \quad 16$$
$$+ \boxed{} \qquad + \boxed{}$$
$$\overline{} \quad \overline{}$$
$$\boxed{} = g \qquad Subtract.$$

Check: $31 = g - 16$

$$31 \overset{?}{=} \boxed{} - 16 \qquad Substitute \ \boxed{} \ for \ g.$$

$$31 \overset{?}{=} \boxed{} \qquad Subtract \ on \ the \ right \ side.$$

TRY THIS!

Solve each equation.

3a. $x - 16 = 72$

$x = $ _____

3b. $h - \frac{1}{2} = \frac{3}{4}$

$h = $ _____

3c. $t - 17 = 84$

$t = $ _____

3d. How do you know whether to add or subtract on both sides when solving an equation?

_____

_____

PRACTICE

Solve each equation.

1. $t + 6 = 10$

$t =$ _____

2. $a + 7 = 15$

$a =$ _____

3. $x - 16 = 72$

$x =$ _____

4. $d - 125 = 55$

$d =$ _____

5. $w + 87 = 102$

$w =$ _____

6. $k + 13 = 61$

$k =$ _____

7. $h + 6.9 = 11.4$

$h =$ _____

8. $y + 2.3 = 10.5$

$y =$ _____

9. $82 + p = 122$

$p =$ _____

10. $n + \frac{1}{2} = \frac{7}{4}$

$n =$ _____

11. $z - \frac{2}{3} = \frac{3}{5}$

$z =$ _____

12. $19 + m = 29$

$m =$ _____

13. $16 = q - 125$

$q =$ _____

14. $9.6 = 5.6 + g$

$g =$ _____

15. $r - 8 = 56$

$r =$ _____

For 16–18, write and solve an equation to answer each question.

16. Kim bought a poster that cost $8.95 and some colored pencils. The total cost was $21.35. How much did the colored pencils cost?

_____

17. The Acme Car Company sold 37 vehicles in June. How many compact cars were sold in June?

_____

_____

Acme Car Company – June Sales	
Type of Car	Number Sold
SUV	8
Compact	?

18. Lindsey finished a race in 58.4 seconds. This was 2.6 seconds faster than her practice time. What was Lindsey's practice time?

_____

Multiplication and Division Equations

COMMON CORE

CC.6.EE.7

Essential question: *How do you solve equations that contain multiplication or division?*

1 EXPLORE   Multiplication Equations

Deanna has a cookie recipe that requires 12 eggs to make 3 batches of cookies. How many eggs are needed per batch of cookies?

Let x represent the number of eggs needed.

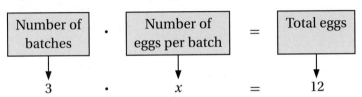

To answer this question, you can use algebra tiles to solve $3x = 12$.

A Model $3x = 12$.

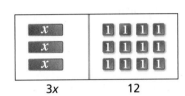

$3x$ 12

B There are 3 variable tiles, so draw circles to separate the tiles into 3 equal groups. One group has been circled for you.

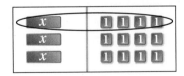

C How many unit tiles are in each group? _____ This is the solution of the equation.

_____ eggs are needed per batch of cookies.

TRY THIS!

1. Caroline ran 15 miles in 5 days. She ran the same distance each day. Write and solve an equation to determine the number of miles she ran each day.

_____

Separating the tiles on both sides of an equation mat into an equal number of groups models dividing both sides of an equation by the same number.

> ### Division Property of Equality
>
> You can divide both sides of an equation by the same nonzero number, and the two sides will remain equal.

When an equation contains multiplication, solve by dividing both sides of the equation by the same number.

2 EXAMPLE Using the Division Property of Equality

Solve each equation.

A $9a = 54$

What number is multiplied by a? _____

Divide both sides of the equation by this number.

$$\frac{9a}{\boxed{}} = \frac{54}{\boxed{}}$$

$a = \boxed{}$ *Divide.*

Check: $9a = 54$

$$9\left(\boxed{}\right) \stackrel{?}{=} 54 \qquad \textit{Substitute } \boxed{} \textit{ for } a.$$

$$\boxed{} \stackrel{?}{=} 54 \qquad \textit{Multiply on the left side.}$$

B $72 = 3d$

What number is multiplied by d? _____

Divide both sides of the equation by this number.

$$\frac{72}{\boxed{}} = \frac{3d}{\boxed{}}$$

$\boxed{} = d$ *Divide.*

Check: $72 = 3d$

$$72 \stackrel{?}{=} 3\left(\boxed{}\right) \qquad \textit{Substitute } \boxed{} \textit{ for } d.$$

$$72 \stackrel{?}{=} \boxed{} \qquad \textit{Multiply on the right side.}$$

TRY THIS!

Solve each equation.

2a. $3x = 21$

$x =$ _____

2b. $2.5h = 45$

$h =$ _____

2c. $143 = 11y$

$y =$ _____

When an equation contains division, solve by multiplying both sides of the equation by the same number.

> **Multiplication Property of Equality**
>
> You can multiply both sides of an equation by the same number, and the two sides will remain equal.

3 EXAMPLE Using the Multiplication Property of Equality

Solve each equation.

A $\frac{x}{5} = 20$

What number is x divided by? _____
Multiply both sides of the equation by this number.

$$\boxed{} \cdot \frac{x}{5} = \boxed{} \cdot 20$$

$$x = \boxed{} \qquad \textit{Multiply.}$$

Check: $\frac{x}{5} = 20$

$$\frac{\boxed{}}{5} \stackrel{?}{=} 20 \qquad \textit{Substitute } \boxed{} \textit{ for x.}$$

$$\boxed{} \stackrel{?}{=} 20 \qquad \textit{Divide on the left side.}$$

B $15 = \frac{r}{2}$

What number is r divided by? _____
Multiply both sides of the equation by this number.

$$\boxed{} \cdot 15 = \boxed{} \cdot \frac{r}{2}$$

$$\boxed{} = r \qquad \textit{Multiply.}$$

Check: $15 = \frac{r}{2}$

$$15 \stackrel{?}{=} \frac{\boxed{}}{2} \qquad \textit{Substitute } \boxed{} \textit{ for r.}$$

$$15 \stackrel{?}{=} \boxed{} \qquad \textit{Divide on the right side.}$$

Solve each equation.

3a. $\dfrac{y}{9} = 12$ **3b.** $\dfrac{x}{4} = 24$ **3c.** $9 = \dfrac{w}{9}$

$y =$ _____ $x =$ _____ $w =$ _____

REFLECT

3d. One way to solve the equation $4x = 32$ is to divide both sides by 4. Another way to solve this equation is to multiply both sides by _____. (*Hint:* Remember that dividing is the same as multiplying by the reciprocal.)

PRACTICE

Solve each equation.

1. $6c = 18$

$c =$ _____

2. $2a = 14$

$a =$ _____

3. $75 = 15x$

$x =$ _____

4. $25d = 350$

$d =$ _____

5. $9.5w = 76$

$w =$ _____

6. $2.5k = 17.5$

$k =$ _____

7. $805 = 7h$

$h =$ _____

8. $9y = 81$

$y =$ _____

9. $\dfrac{n}{4} = 68$

$n =$ _____

10. $12 = \dfrac{m}{9}$

$m =$ _____

11. $\dfrac{n}{2.4} = 15$

$n =$ _____

12. $\dfrac{z}{64} = 8$

$z =$ _____

For 13–16, write and solve an equation to answer each question.

13. Carmen participated in a read-a-thon. Mr. Cole pledged $4.00 per book and gave Carmen $44. How many books did Carmen read?

_____

14. Lee drove 420 miles and used 15 gallons of gasoline. How many miles did Lee's car travel per gallon of gasoline?

_____

15. Last week Tina worked 38 hours in 5 days. How many hours did she work each day?

_____

16. On some days, Melvin commutes 3.5 hours per day to the city for business meetings. Last week he commuted for a total of 14 hours. How many days did he commute to the city?

_____

Equations, Tables, and Graphs

COMMON
CORE

CC.6.EE.9

Essential question: *How can you use equations, tables, and graphs to represent relationships between two variables?*

1 EXPLORE   Equations in Two Variables

Tina is buying DVDs from an online store. Each DVD costs $8, and there is a flat fee of $6 for shipping.

Let x represent the number of DVDs that Tina buys. Let y represent Tina's total cost. An equation in two variables can represent the relationship between x and y.

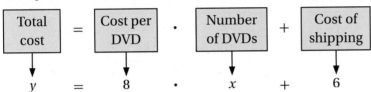

$$y = 8 \cdot x + 6$$

Complete the table.

DVDs Bought x	$8x + 6$	Total Cost y ($)
1	$8(1) + 6$	14
2	$8() + 6$	
3	$8() + 6$	
4	$8() + 6$	
5	$8() + 6$	
6	$8() + 6$	
7	$8() + 6$	

REFLECT

1a. Look at the y-values in the right column of the table. What pattern do you see? What does this pattern mean in the problem?

_____

_____

1b. A *solution of an equation in two variables* is an ordered pair (x, y) that makes the equation true. The ordered pair $(1, 14)$ is a solution of $y = 8x + 6$. Write the other solutions from the table as ordered pairs.

_____

In **1**, the number of DVDs Tina buys determines the total cost. The total cost is the **dependent variable** because it *depends on* the number of DVDs. The number of DVDs is the **independent variable**.

To find the cost of x DVDs, you substituted a value of x into $8x + 6$. The value substituted into the expression is the **input**. You then evaluate the expression to find the value of y, the **output**.

Many real-world situations involve two variable quantities in which one quantity depends on the other. These relationships may be represented by an equation, a table, or a graph.

2 EXPLORE   Variable Relationships

A freight train moves at a constant speed. The distance y in miles that the train has traveled after x hours is shown in the table.

Time x (h)	0	1	2	3
Distance y (mi)	0	50	100	150

A What are the two quantities in this situation?

_____

Which of these quantities depends on the other?

_____

What is the independent variable? _____

What is the dependent variable? _____

B How far does the train travel each hour? _____

Use this number to write an equation in two variables that describes the distance traveled by the train.

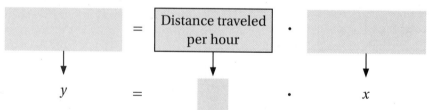

What is the input? _____

What is the output? _____

REFLECT

2a. Use the equation from **B** to find the distance the train travels in 6 hours. _____

2b. Will the train travel 225 miles in 4 hours? Explain.

_____

3 EXAMPLE Graphing Solutions

In **2**, you wrote the equation $y = 50x$ to describe the distance traveled by a train. Graph the solutions to this equation.

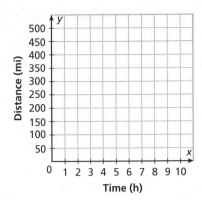

Write ordered pairs to represent the solutions to this equation that are given in the table in **2**.

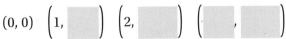

$(0, 0)$ $\left(1, \boxed{}\right)$ $\left(2, \boxed{}\right)$ $\left(\boxed{}, \boxed{}\right)$

Graph these ordered pairs on the coordinate plane.

Connect the ordered pairs with a line. Extend the line to the right beyond your ordered pairs. Every point on this line is a solution to $y = 50x$. In other words, this line represents all solutions to $y = 50x$.

REFLECT

3a. Are there any other ordered pair solutions to the equation? If so, how can you find them? Where will the points be located in the coordinate plane?

_____

_____

3b. Find three more ordered pair solutions and graph them on the coordinate plane.

_____

3c. What do the points between $(0, 0)$ and $(1, 50)$ represent?

_____

_____

3d. Why is the graph not extended past $(0, 0)$ on the left?

_____

_____

TRY THIS!

3e. Use the table to record solutions to the equation $y = x + 2$. Write the solutions as ordered pairs and graph the ordered pairs. Then graph all of the solutions to this equation.

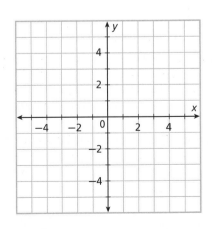

x	−2	−1	0	1	2	3
$y = x + 2$	0	1				

Ordered pairs: $(-2, 0)$, $(-1, 1)$,

_____

Ship to Shore rents paddleboats for a fee of $10 plus an additional $5 per hour that the boat is rented.

1a. Let *x* represent the number of hours a paddleboat is rented, and let *y* represent the total cost of the rental. Complete the equation to show the relationship between *x* and *y*.

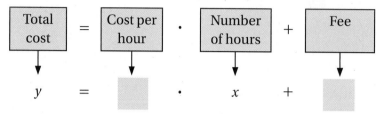

$$y = \boxed{} \cdot x + \boxed{}$$

b. What is the input? _____

c. What is the output? _____

2a. What are the two quantities in this situation? _____

b. Which of these quantities depends on the other? _____

c. What is the independent variable? _____

d. What is the dependent variable? _____

3. Complete the table.

Time Rented x (h)	1	2	3	4	5	6
Total Cost y ($)						

4. Write the ordered pairs from the table.

_____

5. Graph the ordered pairs on the coordinate plane. Connect the points and extend the line to the right.

6a. What is the cost to rent a paddleboat for 8 hours?

_____

b. The cost to rent a paddleboat for 8 hours is represented on the graph by the point _____.

7. The cost to rent a paddleboat for _____ hours is $60. This is represented on the graph by the point _____.

8. Describe two ways to find the cost to rent a paddleboat for 9 hours.

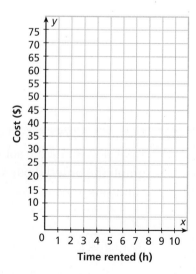

1. _____

2. _____

Solutions of Inequalities

COMMON
CORE

CC.6.EE.5
CC.6.EE.6
CC.6.EE.8

Essential question: *How can you represent solutions of inequalities?*

You have seen the symbols > and < used in inequalities.

- The symbol > means _____.
- The symbol < means _____.

Two additional symbols used in inequalities are ≥ and ≤.

- The symbol ≥ means "is greater than or equal to".
- The symbol ≤ means "is less than or equal to".

1 EXPLORE Inequalities with Variables

A The lowest temperature ever recorded in Florida was −2 °F.
Graph this temperature on the number line.

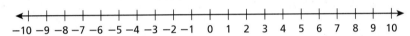

−10 −9 −8 −7 −6 −5 −4 −3 −2 −1 0 1 2 3 4 5 6 7 8 9 10

B The temperatures 0 °F, 3 °F, 6 °F, 5 °F, and −1 °F have also been recorded in Florida.
Graph these temperatures on the number line.

C How do the temperatures in **B** compare to −2?

_____

How can you see this relationship on the number line?

_____

D How many other numbers have the same relationship to −2 as the
temperatures in **B** ? Give some examples.

_____

E Suppose you could graph all of the possible answers to **D** on a number line.
What would the graph look like?

_____

Let the variable *x* represent any of the possible answers to **D** .

Complete this inequality: *x* [   ] −2

When an inequality contains a variable, a solution of that inequality is any
value of the variable that makes the inequality true. For example, 7 is a solution
of $x > -2$, since $7 > -2$ is a true statement. In **1** , the numbers you listed
in **D** are solutions of the inequality $x > -2$.

This number line shows the solutions of $x > -2$:

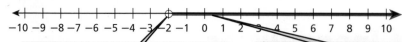

| An *empty* circle means the number *is not* included in the solution. -2 is **not** a solution of $x > -2$. | Shade the number line to the right of -2 to indicate all numbers greater than -2. The arrowhead means that the shaded region extends indefinitely. |

This number line shows the solutions of $x \geq -2$:

| A *solid* circle means the number *is* included in the solution. -2 is a solution of $x \geq -2$. | Shade the number line to the right of -2 to indicate all numbers greater than -2. The arrowhead means that the shaded region extends indefinitely. |

2 EXAMPLE   Graphing Inequalities

Graph the solutions of each inequality.

A $y \leq -3$

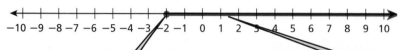

Step 1 Draw a circle at -3.

Is -3 a solution of $y \leq -3$? _____

Will you draw an empty circle or a solid circle? _____

Step 2 Shade the number line.

The variable y represents numbers less than or equal to -3. Where are numbers less than -3 located on the number line?

_____

B $w > 2$

Step 1 Draw a circle at 2.

Is 2 a solution of $w > 2$? _____

Will you draw an empty circle or a solid circle? _____

Step 2 Shade the number line.

The variable w represents numbers greater than 2. Where are these numbers located on the number line?

_____

C $-5 > m$

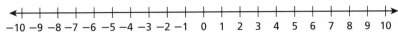

Step 1 Draw a circle at -5.

Is -5 a solution of $-5 > m$? _____

Will you draw an empty circle or a solid circle? _____

Step 2 Shade the number line.

The variable m represents numbers _____ than -5. Where
are these numbers located on the number line? _____

REFLECT

2a. Rewrite the inequality from C with m on the left: m [   ] -5

2b. How is $x < 5$ different from $x \leq 5$?

_____

_____

2c. When graphing an inequality that contains $>$ or $<$, use a(n) _____ circle.
When graphing an inequality that contains $\geq$ or $\leq$, use a(n) _____ circle.

TRY THIS!

Graph the solutions of each inequality.

2d. $t \leq -4$
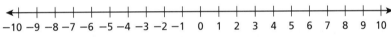

2e. $4 < x$
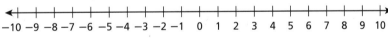

3 **E X A M P L E**   Representing Real-World Situations with Inequalities

**There are at least 5 gallons of water in an aquarium. Write and graph
an inequality to represent this situation.**

Step 1 Write the inequality.

Let g represent the amount of water in gallons.

Can there be 5 gallons of water in the aquarium? _____

Can there be more than 5 gallons of water in the aquarium? _____

Can there be less than 5 gallons of water in the aquarium? _____

The inequality is g [   ] 5.

Step 2 Graph the inequality.

Draw a(n) _____ circle at _____.

Shade the number line to the _____.

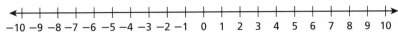

Write and graph an inequality to represent each situation.

3a. Megan must run a mile in 6 minutes or less to beat her best time. _____

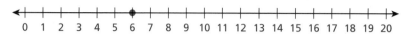

3b. The temperature today will rise above 2 °F. _____

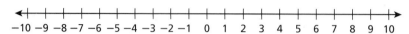

PRACTICE

1. Which numbers in the set $\left\{-5, 0.03, -1, 0, 1.5, -6, \frac{1}{2}\right\}$ are solutions of $x \geq 0$?

_____

Graph each inequality.

2. $t \leq 8$

3. $-7 < h$

4. $x \geq -9$

5. A child must be at least 48 inches tall to ride a roller coaster.

   a. Write and graph an inequality to represent this situation. _____

   b. Can a child who is 46 inches tall ride the roller coaster? Explain.

_____

Write and graph an inequality to represent each situation.

6. There are fewer than 15 students in the cafeteria. _____

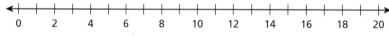

7. No more than 150 people can be seated at the restaurant. _____

8. At least 20 students must sign up for the field trip. _____

9. Shaun can pay at most $50 to have his computer repaired. _____

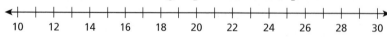

10. The goal of the fundraiser is to raise more than $250. _____

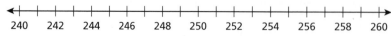

UNIT 4

Problem Solving Connections

COMMON
CORE

CC.6.EE.5
CC.6.EE.6
CC.6.EE.7
CC.6.EE.8
CC.6.EE.9

Travel Plans Mr. Arimoto has won a seven-day trip to Anchorage, Alaska! The prize package will pay for airfare from his home in New Mexico, as well as his hotel, meals, and activities in Anchorage. Mr. Arimoto must pay for any additional travel expenses, including a rental car. Will $400 be enough to cover these expenses?

1 Equations, Tables, and Graphs

A Before leaving for the trip, Mr. Arimoto reserves a rental car that he will pick up when he arrives in Anchorage. Mr. Arimoto wants a mid-size car with GPS. He is unsure how many days he will rent the car.

Rental Car Costs		
	Per Day	**Extras**
Compact	$18	GPS $20
Mid-Size	$30	Car Seat $12
SUV	$50	XM Radio $25

Let y represent the cost of renting a mid-size car with GPS for x days. Write an equation to describe the relationship between x and y.

$y =$ _____

B Use your equation to complete the table.

Number of Days	1	2	3	4	5
Total Cost ($)					

Write the information in the table as ordered pairs.

_____

What do these ordered pairs represent?

_____

C Graph the solutions of the equation on the coordinate plane.

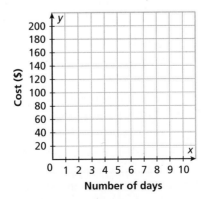

2 Equations and Inequalities

A Mr. Arimoto lives 29 miles from the airport. Write and solve an equation to find the remaining distance to the airport when Mr. Arimoto has driven 14 miles.

B Parking at the airport will cost Mr. Arimoto $9 per day. Use this information to complete the table.

Days	1	2	3	4	5	6	7
Cost ($)							

Let y represent the cost to park for x days. Write an equation that describes the relationship between x and y. $y = $ _____

What is the independent variable? _____

What is the dependent variable? _____

C When Mr. Arimoto arrives at the check-in counter, he sees that there are 3 clerks at the counter and 63 travelers waiting ahead of him. The travelers have formed 3 lines of equal length. Write and solve an equation to find how many travelers are in each line.

D This sign is posted at the check-in counter.

Baggage		
	Maximum Weight per Bag	Cost per Bag
Domestic Flights (U.S.)	50 lb (23 kg)	$25
International	70 lb (32 kg)	$35

Write an inequality to represent the allowable weight of a bag on a domestic flight. How do you know which inequality symbol to use?

_____

Graph the inequality.

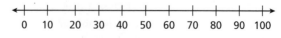

0   10   20   30   40   50   60   70   80   90   100

E While waiting in line, Mr. Arimoto uses his phone to check the weather in Anchorage. The weather report says that today's high temperature will be 2 °F. Write and graph an inequality to show the possible temperatures in Anchorage today.

_____

$$\xleftarrow{\hspace{1cm}}\text{|---|---|---|---|---|---|---|---|---|---|---|---|---|---|---|---|---|---|---|---|}\xrightarrow{\hspace{1cm}}$$
$$-10\ -9\ -8\ -7\ -6\ -5\ -4\ -3\ -2\ -1\ \ 0\ \ 1\ \ 2\ \ 3\ \ 4\ \ 5\ \ 6\ \ 7\ \ 8\ \ 9\ \ 10$$

F Mr. Arimoto is traveling on an airplane that has 12 seats in first class and 150 seats in coach. There are 3 rows of seating in first class. Write and solve an equation to find the number of seats in each first-class row.

G There are 25 rows of seating in coach. Write and solve an equation to determine the number of seats in each row.

H On the flight, Mr. Arimoto purchases a cup of coffee and a blueberry muffin for $8.79. He pays with a $10 bill. Write and solve an equation to determine the amount of change he will receive.

I The airline is showing a movie that is 97 minutes long. Mr. Arimoto falls asleep before the movie starts and misses the first 48 minutes of the movie. Write and solve an equation to determine the amount of time left in the movie when Mr. Arimoto wakes.

3 Answer the Question

Use some of your answers from previous questions to complete the following. You may also have to perform additional calculations.

A Mr. Arimoto takes two bags on his trip. Find the cost for his baggage.

B Mr. Arimoto returns his rental car after 7 days. Explain how to find the total cost of the rental car. What is the total cost of the rental car?

C A snowstorm in Anchorage delays Mr. Arimoto's return home by 2 days. How much will he pay for parking at the airport when he returns to New Mexico?

D Complete the table. Is $400 enough to pay for Mr. Arimoto's travel expenses not covered by his prize package?

Item	Cost ($)
Car rental	
Parking	
Luggage	
In-flight snack	
Total	

Name _____ Class _____ Date _____

MULTIPLE CHOICE

1. Miguel and his team must answer the following question correctly in order to win a quiz bowl contest.

A sunflower grows 5 inches every month. How many months will it take for the sunflower to reach a height of 60 inches?

Which equation can be used to solve this problem?

A. $m + 5 = 60$ **C.** $5m = 60$

B. $m - 5 = 60$ **D.** $\frac{m}{5} = 60$

2. Look at the model.

What is the value of x?

F. 3 **H.** 10

G. 7 **J.** 13

3. Leon had some change in his pocket. Then a friend loaned him $0.25. Now Leon has $1.45 in his pocket. Which equation can be used to find the original amount of money m that Leon had in his pocket?

A. $m + 0.25 = 1.45$

B. $1.45 = m - 0.25$

C. $m + 1.45 = 0.25$

D. $m = 1.45(0.25)$

4. Last week Randy worked 42 hours in 5 days. Which equation could Randy use to find the average number of hours he worked each day?

F. $\frac{h}{5} = 42$ **H.** $\frac{h}{42} = 5$

G. $5h = 42$ **J.** $42h = 5$

5. Look at the model.

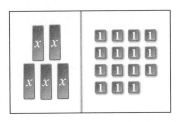

What is the value of x?

A. 3 **C.** 10

B. 5 **D.** 15

6. Solve the equation $x - 4.5 = 17$.

F. $x = 3.8$ **H.** $x = 21.5$

G. $x = 12.5$ **J.** $x = 76.5$

7. Eight batches of pancakes can be made with 16 eggs. How many eggs are needed for one batch of pancakes?

A. 2 eggs **C.** 8 eggs

B. 4 eggs **D.** 24 eggs

8. Jenna's basketball team scored 54 points in its last game. Jenna scored 18 of the points. Which equation could be used to determine the number of points p scored by Jenna's teammates?

F. $18p = 54$ **H.** $p - 18 = 54$

G. $\frac{54}{p} = 18$ **J.** $p + 18 = 54$

9. Lucinda is arranging 150 patio blocks to build a patio. Let p represent the number of patio blocks Lucinda arranged in one hour. Which equation describes the relationship between p and h, the total number of hours Lucinda needed to arrange all 150 patio blocks?

A. $h = 150 + p$ **C.** $h = 150p$

B. $h = \frac{150}{p}$ **D.** $h = 150 - p$

10. Ella builds butterfly houses. The table shows the number of nails n needed to build b butterfly houses.

Butterfly Houses

Number of Houses b	Number of Nails n
2	24
3	36
4	48
5	60
6	72

Which equation describes the relationship between butterfly houses and nails shown in the table?

F. $12b = n$ **H.** $12 - b = n$

G. $12 + b = n$ **J.** $\frac{b}{12} = n$

11. Which graph represents the statement "the temperature will be greater than $-4\ °F$"?

A.
−5 −4 −3 −2 −1   0   1   2   3   4   5

B.
−5 −4 −3 −2 −1   0   1   2   3   4   5

C.
−5 −4 −3 −2 −1   0   1   2   3   4   5

D.
−5 −4 −3 −2 −1   0   1   2   3   4   5

FREE RESPONSE

12. Maria has a newspaper route. She earns $8 per week plus an additional $0.50 for each newspaper that she delivers.

a. Write an equation to describe the total amount y that Maria earns for delivering x newspapers in a week.

_____

b. Use your equation to find the amount of money Maria will earn for a week in which she delivers 30 newspapers.

_____

The graph describes the motion of a car. Use the graph for 13–18.

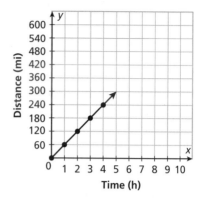

13. What are the two quantities in this situation?

_____

14. Identify the independent and dependent variables.

_____

_____

15. Use the graph to complete the table.

Time x (h)	Distance y (mi)
1	
2	
3	
4	

16. Write an equation that gives the distance the car travels y in x hours.

_____

17. Use your equation to find the distance the car travels in 3.5 hours.

_____

18. Suppose you extend the graph so that it passes through the point $(8, a)$. What is the value of a? What does this point represent?

_____

_____

_____

Ratios and Proportional Relationships

Unit Focus

In this unit you will learn about ratios. You will learn about and use special kinds of ratios, such as rates, percents, and conversion factors.

Unit at a Glance

COMMON CORE

Unpacking the Common Core Standards

Use the table to help you understand the Standards for Mathematical Content that are taught in this unit. Refer to the lessons listed after each standard for exploration and practice.

COMMON CORE Standards for Mathematical Content	What It Means For You
CC.6.RP.1 Understand the concept of a ratio and use ratio language to describe a ratio relationship between two quantities. Lesson 5-1	You will learn how to write ratios to compare two numbers.
CC.6.RP.2 Understand the concept of a unit rate a/b associated with a ratio $a:b$ with $b \neq 0$, and use rate language in the context of a ratio relationship. Lesson 5-3	You will learn how to write and calculate unit rates.
CC.6.RP.3a Make tables of equivalent ratios relating quantities with whole number measurements, find missing values in the tables, and plot the pairs of values on the coordinate plane. Use tables to compare ratios. Lessons 5-1, 5-2	You will make and use tables and graphs that represent ratios.
CC.6.RP.3b Solve unit rate problems including those involving unit pricing and constant speed. Lesson 5-3	You will solve problems involving unit rates and unit prices.
CC.6.RP.3c Find a percent of a quantity as a rate per 100 (e.g., 30% of a quantity means 30/100 times the quantity); solve problems involving finding the whole, given a part and the percent. Lessons 5-4, 5-5	You will solve real-world problems involving percents, and you will find a percent of a number. You will learn the relationship between the percent, the part, and the whole.
CC.6.RP.3d Use ratio reasoning to convert measurement units; manipulate and transform units appropriately when multiplying or dividing quantities. Lesson 5-6	You will convert between customary and metric measurements using a conversion factor.

UNIT 5

Ratios

Essential question: *How do you write ratios and equivalent ratios?*

A **ratio** is a comparison of two numbers by division. The two numbers in a ratio are called *terms*. A ratio can be written in several different ways:

5 dogs to 3 cats   5 to 3   5:3 $\frac{5}{3}$

1 EXAMPLE   Writing Ratios

A The party mix recipe requires _____ cup(s) of pretzels and _____ cup(s) of bagel chips. Write the ratio of pretzels to bagel chips in three different ways.

_____

B The recipe makes a total of _____ cups of party mix. Write the ratio of pretzels to total party mix in three different ways.

_____

Party Mix
Makes 8 cups
4 cups pretzels
2 cups bagel chips
1 cup cheese crackers
1 cup peanuts

TRY THIS!

Write each ratio in three different ways.

1a. bagel chips to peanuts _____

1b. total party mix to pretzels _____

1c. cheese crackers to peanuts _____

REFLECT

1d. What does it mean when the terms in a ratio are equal?

_____

1e. The ratio of floor seats to balcony seats in a theater is 20:1. Does this theater have more floor seats or more balcony seats? How do you know?

_____

1f. At another theater, the ratio of floor seats to balcony seats is 20:19. How do the number of floor seats and the number of balcony seats compare at this theater?

_____

Equivalent ratios are ratios that name the same comparison. Find equivalent ratios by multiplying or dividing both terms of a ratio by the same number.

$$\frac{2}{7} \xrightarrow[\times 2]{\times 2} = \frac{4}{14} \qquad \frac{8}{24} \xrightarrow[\div 4]{\div 4} = \frac{2}{6}$$

2 EXPLORE   Equivalent Ratios

You are in charge of making punch for an upcoming school dance. The punch recipe makes 5 cups of punch by mixing 3 cups of cranberry juice with 2 cups of apple juice.

A What is the ratio of cranberry juice to apple juice? _____

Do you think the punch will taste more like cranberry juice or more like apple juice? Explain.

_____

B You must increase the recipe to serve a large number of people. Fill in the boxes to find the ratio of cranberry juice to apple juice when the recipe is doubled and tripled.

$$\frac{3}{2} \xrightarrow[\times 2]{\times 2} = \boxed{} \qquad \frac{3}{2} \xrightarrow[\times 3]{\times 3} = \boxed{}$$

To double the recipe, you need _____ cups of cranberry juice and _____ cups of apple juice. This makes a total of _____ cups of punch.

To triple the recipe, you need _____ cups of cranberry juice and _____ cups of apple juice. This makes a total of _____ cups of punch.

C The ratios you found in **B** are equivalent to $\frac{3}{2}$. Find three other ratios that are equivalent to $\frac{3}{2}$. _____

D How much of each juice would you need to make a total of 40 cups of punch? _____

TRY THIS!
Complete each pair of equivalent ratios.

2a. $\frac{5}{6} = \frac{\boxed{}}{24}$ **2b.** $\frac{1}{4} = \frac{8}{\boxed{}}$ **2c.** $\frac{30}{6} = \frac{\boxed{}}{3}$

Find three ratios equivalent to the given ratio.

2d. $\frac{6}{8}$ _____ **2e.** $\frac{24}{18}$ _____ **2f.** $\frac{15}{10}$ _____

2g. Why can you multiply or divide both terms of a ratio by the same number without changing the value of the ratio?

_____

_____

3 EXPLORE **Comparing Ratios**

Anna's recipe for lemonade calls for 2 cups of lemon juice and 3 cups of water. Bailey's recipe calls for 3 cups of lemon juice and 5 cups of water.

A In Anna's recipe, the ratio of lemon juice to water is _____.
Complete the table with equivalent ratios.

		$2 \cdot 2$	$2 \cdot$	$2 \cdot$
Lemon Juice (c)	2	4		
Water (c)	3		9	15
		$3 \cdot 2$	$3 \cdot 3$	$3 \cdot 5$

B In Bailey's recipe, the ratio of lemon juice to water is _____.
Complete the table with equivalent ratios.

		$3 \cdot 3$	$3 \cdot 4$	$3 \cdot$
Lemon Juice (c)	3	9	12	
Water (c)	5			25
		$5 \cdot 3$	$5 \cdot$	$5 \cdot$

C In each table, there is a column in which the amount of water is the same. Circle these columns in the tables.

D Examine these two columns. Whose recipe makes stronger lemonade? How do you know?

_____

_____

E The ratio of lemon juice to water in the stronger recipe is _____ than the ratio of lemon juice to water in the other recipe.

Write inequality symbols to compare the ratios: $\frac{10}{15}$ ▢ $\frac{9}{15}$

$\frac{2}{3}$ ▢ $\frac{3}{5}$

3a. Describe another way to determine which recipe makes stronger lemonade.

_____

_____

_____

3b. **Error Analysis** Marisol said, "Bailey's lemonade is stronger because it has more lemon juice. Bailey's lemonade has 3 cups of lemon juice, and Anna's lemonade has only 2 cups of lemon juice." Explain why Marisol is incorrect.

_____

_____

PRACTICE

The contents of Dean's pencil box are shown. Write each ratio in three different ways.

1. pencils to pens _____

2. total items to crayons _____

3. erasers to pencils _____

4. markers to total items _____

Dean's Pencil Box
5 pencils
2 erasers
3 pens
12 markers
24 crayons

Write three ratios equivalent to the given ratio.

5. $\frac{12}{28}$ _____

6. $\frac{5}{2}$ _____

7. $\frac{10}{3}$ _____

8. Aaron's math homework includes the following problem: $\frac{15}{25} = \frac{9}{}$

a. How is this problem different from the problems involving equivalent ratios in this lesson?

_____

b. You can use a table to solve this problem. Complete the table to find the answer to Aaron's homework problem.

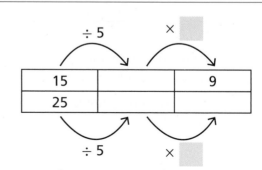

Ratios, Tables, and Graphs

Essential question: *How can you use tables and graphs to understand ratios?*

1 **EXPLORE**   **Finding Ratios from Tables**

The Webster family is taking a train to Washington, D.C. The train travels at a constant speed. The table shows the distance that the train travels in various amounts of time.

Distance (mi)	120	150		240	
Time (h)	2		3		5

A   Use the numbers in the first column of the table to write a ratio of distance to time._____

B   How far does the train travel in one hour? _____
Use your answer to write another ratio of distance to time. _____

C   The ratios in **A** and **B** are _____.

D   How can you use your answer to **B** to find the distance the train travels in a given number of hours?

_____

E   Complete the table. What are the equivalent ratios shown in the table?

$$\frac{120}{2} = \frac{150}{\;\;\;} = \frac{\;\;\;}{\;\;\;} = \frac{\;\;\;}{\;\;\;} = \frac{\;\;\;}{\;\;\;}$$

REFLECT

1a.   What information given in the problem explains why all of the ratios are equivalent? _____

1b.   What is the train's speed? _____

Write the train's speed as a ratio. $\dfrac{\boxed{}\text{ miles}}{1 \text{ hour}}$

How is this ratio related to the ratios in **E** ? _____

1c.   When the time increases by 1 hour, the distance increases by _____ miles.
The distance traveled in 5 hours is _____ miles, so the distance traveled in 6 hours is _____ miles.

A Copy the table from **1** that shows the time and distance information for the train.

Distance (mi)	120	150		240	
Time (h)	2		3		5

B Write the information in the table as ordered pairs. Use Time as the *x*-coordinates and Distance as the *y*-coordinates.

$(2, 120) \left(\boxed{}, 150 \right) \left(3, \boxed{} \right) \left(\boxed{}, 240 \right) \left(5, \boxed{} \right)$

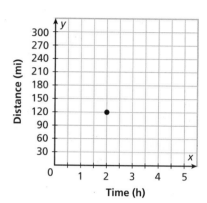

Graph the ordered pairs and connect the points.

Describe your graph. _____

C For each ordered pair that you graphed, write the ratio of

the *y*-coordinate to the *x*-coordinate. _____

D The train's speed is $\dfrac{\boxed{}\ \text{miles}}{1\ \text{hour}}$. How are the ratios in **C** related to the train's

speed? _____

E The point (3.5, 210) is on the graph but not in the table. The ratio of the

y-coordinate to the *x*-coordinate is $\dfrac{\boxed{}}{\boxed{}}$. How is this ratio related to the ratios

in **C** and **D** ? _____

So, in 3.5 hours, the train travels _____ miles.

F **Conjecture** What do you think is true about every point on the graph?

_____

_____

2a. How can you use the graph to find the distance the train travels in 4.5 hours?

_____

_____

2b. If the graph were continued further, would the point (7, 420) be on the

graph? How do you know? _____

Unit Rates

Essential question: *How can you use unit rates to solve problems and make comparisons?*

COMMON CORE

CC.6.RP.2
CC.6.RP.3b

1 EXPLORE Comparing Prices

Shana is at the grocery store comparing two brands of juice. Brand A costs $3.84 for a 16-ounce bottle. Brand B costs $4.50 for a 25-ounce bottle.

To compare the costs, Shana must compare prices for equal amounts of juice. How can she do this?

A Complete the tables.

BRAND A	
Ounces	Price ($)
16	3.84
8	1.92
4	
2	
1	

÷ 2 ... ÷ 2

BRAND B	
Ounces	Price ($)
25	4.50
5	
1	

÷ 5 ... ÷ 5

B Brand A costs $ _____ per ounce. Brand B costs $ _____ per ounce.

C Which brand is the better buy? Why? _____

REFLECT

1a. Describe another method to compare the costs.

_____

_____

TRY THIS!

1b. Abby can buy an 8-pound bag of dog food for $7.40 or a 4-pound bag of the same dog food for $5.38. Which is the better buy? _____

A **rate** is a ratio of two quantities that have different units. A **unit rate** is a rate in which the second quantity is one unit. When the first quantity in a unit rate is an amount of money, the unit rate is sometimes called a *unit price* or *unit cost*.

2 EXAMPLE Calculating Unit Rates

A **Maria pays $60 for 5 music lessons. What is the cost per lesson?**

Use the information in the problem to write a rate: $\dfrac{\$60}{5 \text{ lessons}}$

To find the unit rate, divide both quantities in the rate by the same number so that the second quantity is 1:

$$\dfrac{\$60}{5 \text{ lessons}} \overset{\div}{\underset{\div}{=}} \implies \dfrac{\$\boxed{}}{1 \text{ lesson}}$$

Maria's music lessons cost $ _____ per lesson.

B **The cost of 3 candles is $19.50. What is the unit price?**

$$\dfrac{\$19.50}{3 \text{ candles}} \overset{\div}{\underset{\div}{=}} \implies \dfrac{\$\boxed{}}{1 \text{ candle}}$$

The unit price is $ _____ per candle.

C **Michael walks 30 meters in 20 seconds. How many meters does Michael walk per second?**

$$\dfrac{30 \text{ meters}}{20 \text{ seconds}} \overset{\div}{\underset{\div}{=}} \implies \dfrac{\boxed{} \text{ meters}}{1 \text{ second}}$$

Michael walks _____ meters per second.

D **A bakery charges $7 for $\frac{1}{2}$ dozen muffins. What is the price per dozen?**

Use the information in the problem to write a rate: $\dfrac{\$7}{\frac{1}{2} \text{ dozen}}$

In this rate, the second quantity is less than 1. To find the unit rate, *multiply* both quantities by the same number so that the second unit is 1:

$$\dfrac{\$7}{\frac{1}{2} \text{ dozen}} \overset{\times}{\underset{\times}{=}} \implies \dfrac{\$\boxed{}}{1 \text{ dozen}}$$

The muffins cost $ _____ per dozen.

TRY THIS!

2a. There are 156 players on 13 teams. How many players are on each team?
_____ players per team

2b. A package of 36 photographs costs $18. What is the cost per photograph?
$ _____ per photograph

REFLECT

2c. In all of these problems, how is the unit rate related to the rate given in the original problem? _____

3 **E X A M P L E**   **Problem-Solving with Unit Rates**

A In a youth soccer league, each team will have 18 players and 3 coaches. This year, 162 players signed up to play soccer. How many coaches are needed?

Method 1 Find the unit rate. How many players per coach?

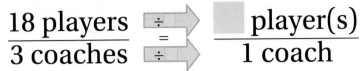

There are _____ players per coach.

$$\frac{162 \text{ players}}{\boxed{}\ \text{players per coach}} = \boxed{} \text{ coaches}$$

Method 2 Use equivalent ratios.

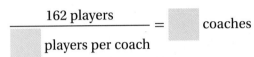

The soccer league needs _____ coaches.

B Tim can mow 4 lawns in 6 hours. How many lawns can he mow in 15 hours?

Find the unit rate.

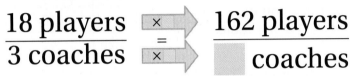

How can you use the unit rate to find how many lawns Tim can mow in 15 hours?

_____

Tim can mow _____ lawns in 15 hours.

TRY THIS!

3a. On Tuesday, Donovan earned $9 for 2 hours of babysitting. On Saturday, he babysat for the same family and earned $31.50. How many hours did he babysit on Saturday? _____ hours

REFLECT

3b. How could you use estimation to check that your answer to **3a** is reasonable?

_____

_____

The sizes and prices of three brands of laundry detergent are shown in the table. Use the table for 1 and 2.

Brand	Size (oz)	Price ($)
A	32	4.80
B	48	5.76
C	128	17.92

1. What is the unit price for each detergent?

   Brand A: $ _____ per ounce

   Brand B: $ _____ per ounce

   Brand C: $ _____ per ounce

2. Which detergent is the best buy? _____

Mason's favorite brand of peanut butter is available in two sizes. Each size and its price are shown in the table. Use the table for 3 and 4.

	Size (oz)	Price ($)
Regular	16	3.36
Family Size	40	7.60

3. What is the unit rate for each size of peanut butter?

   Regular: $ _____ per ounce

   Family size: $ _____ per ounce

4. Which size is the better buy? _____

For 5 and 6, find the unit rate.

5. Lisa walked 48 blocks in 3 hours.

   _____ blocks per hour

6. Gordon can type 1,800 words in 25 minutes.

   _____ words per minute

7. A particular frozen yogurt has 75 calories in 2 ounces. How many calories are in 8 ounces of the yogurt? _____ calories

8. The cost of 10 oranges is $1.00. What is the cost of 5 dozen oranges? $ _____

9. A carpenter installed 10 windows in 4 hours. Another carpenter installed 50 windows in 20 hours. Are the two carpenters working at the same rate? Explain.

   _____

   _____

Percents

Essential question: *How are percents related to fractions and decimals?*

COMMON
CORE

CC.6.RP.3c

1 EXPLORE — Fractions and Decimals

The free-throw ratios for three basketball players are shown.

Player 1: $\frac{17}{25}$ Player 2: 0.72   Player 3: $\frac{14}{20}$

A For each player, shade the grid to represent his free-throw ratio.

Player 1   Player 2   Player 3

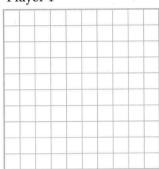 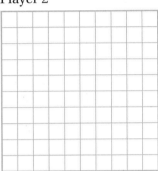 

B Which player has the greatest free-throw ratio? _____

How is this shown on the grids?

_____

C Write the free-throw ratios in order from least to greatest.

_____

REFLECT

1. How did you determine how many squares to shade on each grid?

_____

_____

_____

A **percent** is a ratio that compares a number to 100. The symbol % is used to show a percent.

17% is equivalent to: 62.5% is equivalent to:

- $\frac{17}{100}$ • $\frac{62.5}{100}$
- 17 to 100   • 62.5 to 100
- 17:100   • 62.5:100

A **Write 15% as a fraction in simplest form.**

Step 1 Write the percent as a fraction with a denominator of 100.

$$15\% = \frac{15}{\boxed{}}$$

Step 2 Simplify the fraction.

What is the GCF of 15 and 100? _____

Divide the numerator and the denominator by the GCF.

$$\frac{15}{100} = \frac{15 \div \boxed{}}{100 \div \boxed{}} = \frac{\boxed{}}{\boxed{}}$$

B **Write 15% as a decimal.**

Step 1 Write the percent as a fraction with a denominator of 100.

$$15\% = \frac{15}{\boxed{}}$$

Step 2 Write the fraction as a decimal.

$$15\% = \frac{15}{\boxed{}} = \underline{\hspace{2cm}}$$

C **Write 300% as a fraction in simplest form and as a decimal.**

Fraction Write the percent as a fraction with a denominator of 100. Then simplify.

$$300\% = \frac{\boxed{}}{\boxed{}} = \frac{\boxed{} \div 100}{\boxed{} \div 100} = \frac{\boxed{}}{\boxed{}}$$

Decimal Write the percent as a fraction with a denominator of 100. Then write the fraction as a decimal.

$$300\% = \frac{300}{\boxed{}} = \boxed{}$$

TRY THIS!

Write each percent as a fraction in simplest form and as a decimal.

2a. 10% _____

2b. 85% _____

2c. 3% _____

2d. 450% _____

2e. 38% _____

2f. 95% _____

REFLECT

2g. Why is 100% equal to 1? _____

2h. What is a "shortcut" for writing a percent as a decimal? Give an example.

_____

_____

A Write $\frac{7}{20}$ as a percent.

Method 1 *When the denominator is a factor of 100:*

Write an equivalent fraction with a denominator of 100.

$$\frac{7}{20} = \frac{}{100}$$

Write the percent.

$$\frac{}{100} = \underline{\hspace{2cm}}\%$$

B Write $\frac{3}{8}$ as a percent.

Method 2 *When the denominator is NOT a factor of 100:*

Step 1 Use long division to divide the numerator by the denominator. Add a decimal point and zeros to the right of the numerator as needed.

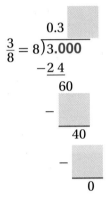

$$\frac{3}{8} = 8\overline{)3.000}$$

Step 2 Write the quotient. Then move the decimal point two places to the right and add a percent symbol.

$$\frac{3}{8} = 0.\boxed{} = \underline{\hspace{2cm}}\%$$

TRY THIS!

Write each fraction as a decimal and as a percent.

3a. $\frac{3}{10}$ _____   **3b.** $\frac{2}{25}$ _____   **3c.** $\frac{7}{50}$ _____

3d. $\frac{12}{30}$ _____   **3e.** $\frac{1}{8}$ _____   **3f.** $\frac{350}{100}$ _____

REFLECT

3g. Moving the decimal point two places to the right is equivalent to performing what operation? _____

3h. A given fraction's numerator is greater than its denominator. When this fraction is written as a percent, what will be true about the percent?

_____

1. At Brian's Bookstore, 0.3 of the shelves hold mysteries, 25% of the shelves hold travel books, and $\frac{7}{20}$ of the shelves hold children's books. Which type of book covers the most shelf space in the bookstore?

_____

Write each percent as a fraction in simplest form and as a decimal.

2. 60%

3. 5%

4. 37%

_____ _____ _____

5. 500%

6. 48%

7. 66%

_____ _____ _____

8. 23%

9. 1%

10. 8%

_____ _____ _____

Write each fraction as a decimal and as a percent.

11. $\frac{27}{50}$

12. $\frac{250}{100}$

13. $\frac{7}{10}$

_____ _____ _____

14. $\frac{24}{30}$

15. $\frac{3}{5}$

16. $\frac{11}{16}$

_____ _____ _____

17. $\frac{9}{20}$

18. $\frac{1}{25}$

19. $\frac{18}{45}$

_____ _____ _____

20. Justine answered 68 questions correctly on an 80-question test.

   a. What percent of the questions did Justine answer correctly? _____

   b. To find the percent of questions that Justine answered incorrectly, subtract your answer to **a** from 100%: 100% − ▢ = ▢

   What percent of the questions did Justine answer incorrectly? _____

21. Graph each fraction or percent on the number line.

   A. $\frac{4}{5}$ **B.** 20%   **C.** $\frac{1}{2}$ **D.** $\frac{6}{8}$

Percent Problems

5-5

Essential question: *How do you use percents to solve problems?*

COMMON CORE

CC.6.RP.3c

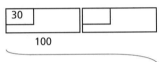 **1 EXPLORE** Finding Percent of a Number

A sporting-goods store received a shipment of 400 baseball gloves, and 30% were left-handed. How many left-handed gloves were in the shipment?

A You can draw a diagram to solve this problem.

30% means 30 out of _____. There were _____ left-handed gloves for every 100 baseball gloves.

Complete the diagram to model this situation.

30	

100

400

REFLECT

1a. Describe how the diagram models the shipment of gloves.

_____

_____

_____

1b. How can you use the diagram to find the total number of left-handed gloves in the shipment?

_____

B You can use a bar model to solve this problem. The bar represents 100%, or the entire shipment of 400 gloves. Divide the bar into 10 equal parts and label each part.

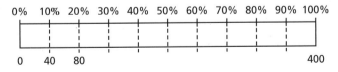

0% 10% 20% 30% 40% 50% 60% 70% 80% 90% 100%

0   40   80   400

REFLECT

1c. How did you determine the labels along the bottom of the bar model?

_____

_____

1d. How can you use the bar model to find the number of left-handed gloves?

_____

When finding the percent of a number, convert the percent to a fraction or decimal and then multiply.

2 EXAMPLE Finding Percent of a Number

A lacrosse team played 30 games and won 80% of the games. How many games did the team win?

To answer this question, you must find 80% of 30.

Method 1 Use a fraction.

Step 1 Write the percent as a fraction in simplest form.

$$80\% = \frac{80}{\boxed{}} = \frac{\boxed{}}{\boxed{}}$$

Step 2 Multiply this fraction by the total number of games.

$$\frac{\boxed{}}{\boxed{}} \cdot 30 = \frac{\boxed{}}{\boxed{}} \cdot \frac{30}{5} = \boxed{}$$

Method 2 Use a decimal.

Step 1 Write the percent as a decimal: $80\% = $ _____

Step 2 Multiply this decimal by the total number of games.

$$\boxed{} \cdot 30 = \boxed{}$$

80% of 30 is _____. The team won _____ games.

TRY THIS!

Find the percent of the number.

2a. 20% of 180

_____

2b. 80% of 40

_____

2c. 75% of 480

_____

2d. 20% of 45

_____

2e. 25% of 16

_____

2f. 90% of 80

_____

REFLECT

2g. When might it be easier to write the percent as a fraction rather than as a decimal? Give an example.

_____

_____

_____

You can use an equation to solve percent problems:

| percent | · | whole | = | part |

A percent problem may ask you to find any of the three pieces of this equation—the percent, the whole, or the part.

3 EXAMPLE   Finding the Whole

A **A girls' softball team has 3 pitchers. The pitchers make up 20% of the team. How many total players are on the softball team?**

Identify the pieces of the percent equation. Use the variable n for any piece that is unknown.

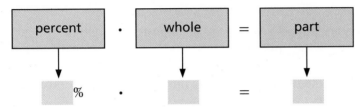

Write the percent as a decimal. _____

Substitute this decimal for the percent and rewrite the equation. _____

Solve the equation.

$\dfrac{0.2n}{\boxed{}} = \dfrac{3}{\boxed{}}$ *Divide both sides by* _____.

$n = \boxed{}$

There are _____ players on the softball team.

B **12% of what number is 45?**

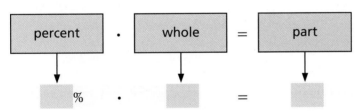

Write the percent as a decimal. _____

Substitute this decimal for the percent and rewrite the equation. _____

Solve the equation.

$\dfrac{0.12n}{\boxed{}} = \dfrac{45}{\boxed{}}$ *Divide both sides by* _____.

$n = \boxed{}$

12% of _____ is 45.

TRY THIS!

3a. 180 is 30% of _____.

3b. 25% of _____ is 40.

PRACTICE

Find the percent of each number.

1. 5% of 30

2. 80% of 80

3. 95% of 260

4. 20% of 90

5. 32% of 50

6. 2% of 350

7. 25% of 56

8. 3% of 600

9. 7% of 200

10. At a shelter, 15% of the dogs are puppies. There are 60 dogs at the shelter. How many are puppies? _____ puppies

11. Terry has a box that originally held 64 crayons. She is missing 25% of the crayons. How many crayons are missing? _____ crayons

12. In a survey, 230 people were asked their favorite color, and 20% of the people surveyed chose blue. How many people chose blue? _____ people

13. Leah is saving money to buy her sister a graduation gift. She needs $44, and she has saved 25% of this amount so far. How much more money must Leah save? $ _____

Complete each sentence.

14. 4% of _____ is 56.

15. 58 is 20% of _____.

16. 35% of _____ is 42.

17. 360 is 24% of _____.

18. 92% of _____ is 115.

19. 9 is 3% of _____.

20. 45 is 20% of _____.

21. 8% of _____ is 2.

22. Use the circle graph to determine how many hours per day Becky spends on each activity.

School: _____ hours

Eating: _____ hours

Sleep: _____ hours

Homework: _____ hours

Free time: _____ hours

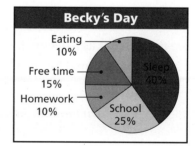

Becky's Day

Eating 10%

Free time 15%

Homework 10%

Sleep 40%

School 25%

Converting Measurements

COMMON
CORE

CC.6.RP.3d

Essential question: *How can you use ratios to convert measurements?*

Measurement is a mathematical tool that people use every day. Measurements are used when determining the length, weight, or capacity of an object.

There are several different systems of measurement. The two most common systems are the *customary system* and the *metric system*.

The table below shows equivalencies between the customary and metric systems. You can use these equivalencies to convert a measurement in one system to a measurement in the other system.

Length	Weight/Mass	Capacity
1 inch = 2.54 centimeters 1 foot ≈ 0.305 meters 1 yard ≈ 0.914 meters 1 mile ≈ 1.61 kilometers	1 ounce ≈ 28.4 grams 1 pound ≈ 0.454 kilograms	1 fluid ounce ≈ 29.6 milliliters 1 quart ≈ 0.946 liter 1 gallon ≈ 3.79 liters

Most conversions are approximate, as indicated by the symbol ≈.

1 EXPLORE Converting Inches to Centimeters

The length of a sheet of a paper is 11 inches. What is this length in centimeters?

You can use a diagram to solve this problem. Each block represents 1 inch.

1 inch = _____ centimeter(s)

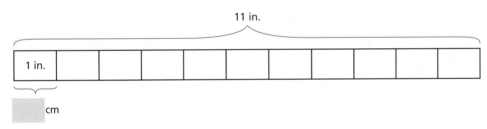

How does the diagram help you solve the problem?

_____

11 inches = _____ centimeters

TRY THIS!

1. Draw a diagram to find approximately how many grams are equivalent to 6 ounces.

6 ounces ≈ _____ grams

Another way to convert measurements is by using a ratio called a *conversion factor*. A **conversion factor** is a ratio of two equivalent measurements. Since the two measurements in a conversion factor are equivalent, a conversion factor is a ratio equivalent to 1.

2 EXAMPLE Using Conversion Factors

A **Vicki put 22 gallons of gasoline in her car. About how many liters of gasoline did she put in her car?**

Step 1 Find the conversion factor.

_____ liter(s) ≈ 1 gallon

Write as a ratio: $\dfrac{\boxed{} \text{ liter(s)}}{1 \text{ gallon}}$

Step 2 Convert the given measurement.

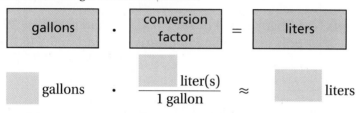

$\boxed{}$ gallons · $\dfrac{\boxed{}\text{ liter(s)}}{1 \text{ gallon}}$ ≈ $\boxed{}$ liters

Vicki put about _____ liters of gasoline in her car.

B **While lifting weights, John adds 11.35 kilograms to his bar. About how many pounds did he add to his bar?**

Step 1 Find the conversion factor.

1 pound ≈ _____ kilogram(s)

Write as a ratio: $\dfrac{1 \text{ pound}}{\boxed{} \text{ kilogram(s)}}$

Step 2 Convert the given measurement.

| kilograms | · | conversion factor | = | pounds |

$\boxed{}$ kilograms · $\dfrac{1 \text{ pound}}{\boxed{}\text{ kilogram(s)}}$ ≈ $\boxed{}$ pounds

John has added about _____ pounds to his bar.

TRY THIS!

2a. 6 quarts ≈ _____ liters

2b. 14 feet ≈ _____ meters

2c. 255.6 grams ≈ _____ ounces

2d. 7 liters ≈ _____ quarts

Yolanda's office is 12 feet long by 8 feet wide. She plans to purchase carpet for the entire office. The carpet costs $15 per square meter. What will be the total cost of the new carpet?

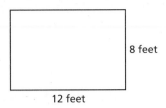

8 feet

12 feet

First find the area of the office in square meters.

Step 1 Convert each measurement to meters.

Length: ⬜ feet · $\dfrac{\boxed{} \text{ meter(s)}}{1 \text{ foot}}$ ≈ ⬜ meter(s)

Width: ⬜ feet · $\dfrac{\boxed{} \text{ meter(s)}}{1 \text{ foot}}$ ≈ ⬜ meter(s)

Step 2 Find the area.

Area = length · width

= ⬜ · ⬜

= ⬜ square meters

Now find the total cost of the carpet.

square meters · cost per square meter = total cost

⬜ · ⬜ = $ ⬜

REFLECT

3a. **Error Analysis** Leo found the area of Yolanda's office in square meters as shown. Explain why Leo's answer is incorrect.

> Area = 12 · 8 = 96 square feet
>
> 96 square feet · $\dfrac{0.305 \text{ meter}}{1 \text{ foot}}$ ≈ 29.28 square meters

_____

_____

TRY THIS!

3b. A flower bed is 6 feet wide and 10 feet long. What is the area of the flower bed in square meters? Round your answer to the nearest hundredth.

_____ square meters

1. A ruler is 12 inches long. What is the length of this ruler in centimeters?
_____ centimeters

2. A bottle contains 4 fluid ounces of medicine. About how many milliliters of medicine are in the bottle? _____ milliliters

3. Miguel rode 19 miles on his bicycle. About how many kilometers did he ride?
_____ kilometers

4. A gas can contains 2.5 gallons of gas. About how many liters of gas are in the gas can?
_____ liters

5. A kitten weighs 4 pounds. About how many kilograms does the kitten weigh?
_____ kilograms

Convert each measurement.

6. 20 yards ≈ _____ meters

7. 12 ounces ≈ _____ grams

8. 5 quarts ≈ _____ liters

9. 30 inches ≈ _____ centimeters

10. 42 feet ≈ _____ meters

11. 7 gallons ≈ _____ liters

12. 5 miles ≈ _____ kilometers

13. 400 meters ≈ _____ yards

14. 165 centimeters ≈ _____ inches

15. 137.25 meters ≈ _____ feet

16. 10 liters ≈ _____ gallons

17. 10,000 kilometers ≈ _____ miles

18. A countertop is 16 feet long and 3 feet wide.

    a. What is the area of the countertop in square meters? _____ square meters

    b. Tile costs $28 per square meter. How much will it cost to cover the countertop with new tile? $ _____

19. Reasoning The length of a particular object is x inches.

    a. Will this object's length in centimeters be greater than x or less than x? Explain.

_____

_____

    b. Will this object's length in meters be greater than x or less than x? Explain.

_____

_____

UNIT 5

Problem Solving Connections

Sweet Success? A youth group is raising money for a ski trip by baking and selling muffins on weekend mornings. The money raised will be distributed evenly among the group members, and the goal is to raise $65 per person. Will the group meet this goal?

COMMON CORE

CC.6.RP.1
CC.6.RP.2
CC.6.RP.3a, b, c, d

1 Making Muffins

Ruth volunteered to make pumpkin muffins for the sale. The ingredients used in Ruth's recipe are shown.

A Write the ratio of total flour to sugar in three different ways.

_____

B Write the ratio of vanilla to molasses. Then write a ratio that is equivalent. Explain how you found the equivalent ratio.

_____

C At the grocery store, Ruth sees that a 15-ounce can of pumpkin costs $1.59 and a 29-ounce can of pumpkin costs $3.05. Which is the better buy?

Pumpkin Muffins
4 cups white flour
4 cups wheat flour
4 tsp baking soda
2 tsp salt
4 tsp cinnamon
2 tsp ginger
1 tsp cloves
3 cups brown sugar
6 tsp molasses
1 cup oil
8 eggs
4 cups pumpkin
4 tsp vanilla
3 cups milk

D Ruth decides to make a larger batch of muffins for the bake sale by increasing the recipe. The increased recipe requires 6 teaspoons of cinnamon. Now Ruth must determine how many eggs she needs.

What is the ratio of cinnamon to eggs in the original recipe? _____

The ratio of cinnamon to eggs in the increased recipe must be _____ to the ratio in the original recipe.

Use the table to help you find the number of eggs that Ruth needs.

Cinnamon (tsp)	4		6
Eggs	8		

Ruth needs _____ eggs.

2 Preparing for the Sale

A   The group has a 6-foot long table and a plastic tablecloth for the sale. The tablecloth's package states that the tablecloth is 180 centimeters long. Is the tablecloth long enough to cover the table? Explain.

Length
1 inch = 2.54 centimeters

B   Allison has painted a large "Muffin Sale" sign to display at the table. Chris wants to paint more signs.

Allison made purple paint by mixing 3 parts red paint with 4 parts blue paint. Chris has 2 fluid ounces of blue paint. To match Allison's shade of purple, how much red paint should Chris mix with his blue paint?

C   The group members price the muffins at $15 per dozen. What is the price per muffin?

3 Sale Results

A   The table shows results after several weekends of sales.

Muffins	Dozens Made	Dozens Sold
Pumpkin	18	17
Blueberry	16	15
Chocolate chip	24	24
Banana nut	14	13

What percent of the muffins made were pumpkin muffins?

B Which type of muffin represents $\frac{1}{3}$ of the muffins made? Explain.

C What percent of the muffins that youth group members made did NOT sell? Round your answer to the nearest percent.

D Which type of muffin was most popular? Justify your answer.

4 Answer the Question

A The treasurer of the youth group tracks the muffin sales for several weeks. Help her complete her spreadsheet.

Muffin Sales				
Type of Muffin	Dozens Made	Dozens Sold	Number of Muffins Sold	Income
Pumpkin	18	17		
Blueberry	16	15		
Chocolate chip	24	24		
Banana	14	13		
			Total Income	

B After tallying the group members' receipts for supplies, the treasurer has calculated that it cost the youth group $3.50 to bake a dozen muffins. How much has it cost the group to bake all of the muffins so far?

C To find the group's profit, subtract cost from income. How much profit has the group earned from muffin sales so far?

D The youth group divides the profit evenly between the 15 members. How much does each member now have toward the cost of the trip? Did the group meet its goal?

E Ruth suggests raising the price per muffin by $0.25 in future sales, saying, "If this had been the price from the beginning, we would have met our goal by now." Is Ruth correct? Explain.

Name _____ Class _____ Date _____

MULTIPLE CHOICE

1. The ratio of boys to girls in a classroom is 15 to 12. What is the ratio of boys to total students in the classroom?

   A. 12:15   **C.** 15:27

   B. 12:27   **D.** 27:15

2. Each day, the cafeteria staff at Brookview Middle School orders 80 pints of white milk and 30 pints of chocolate milk. Which ratio is equivalent to the ratio of white milk to chocolate milk?

   F. 8:11   **H.** 3:8

   G. 8:3   **J.** 3:11

3. A baker makes 5 apple pies for every 3 blueberry pies. Last week the baker made 15 blueberry pies. How many apple pies did the baker make?

   A. 8   **C.** 25

   B. 9   **D.** 40

4. Bagel prices at four different bakeries are shown below. Which is the best buy?

   F. Bakery 1: A dozen bagels costs $7.79.

   G. Bakery 2: 6 bagels cost $4.09.

   H. Bakery 3: Bagels cost $0.75 each.

   J. Bakery 4: 2 bagels cost $1.55.

5. Which is another way to write the ratio 8:3?

   A. 3 to 8   **C.** 8 to 11

   B. $\frac{3}{8}$ **D.** 8 to 3

6. Which is **not** equivalent to $\frac{45}{75}$?

   F. $\frac{9}{15}$ **H.** 60%

   G. $\frac{15}{25}$ **J.** 70%

7. Which shows the ratio "44 to 200" written as a percent, a decimal, and a fraction in simplest form?

   A. 44%, 0.44, $\frac{44}{50}$

   B. 44%, 0.22, $\frac{22}{100}$

   C. 22%, 0.2, $\frac{22}{100}$

   D. 22%, 0.22, $\frac{11}{50}$

8. The length of a poster is 16 inches.

Length
1 inch = 2.54 centimeters

   What is the length of this poster in centimeters?

   F. 6.30 centimeters

   G. 13.46 centimeters

   H. 18.54 centimeters

   J. 40.64 centimeters

9. A certain shade of orange requires a 3 to 2 ratio of yellow to red paint. You have 6 gallons of red paint. How much yellow paint do you need?

   A. 4 gallons

   B. 5 gallons

   C. 9 gallons

   D. 12 gallons

10. Out of 20 athletes surveyed, 10 athletes chose soccer as their favorite sport, 6 chose golf, and the others chose football. What percent of the athletes chose football?

   F. 20%

   G. 30%

   H. 40%

   J. 50%

11. In Miranda's flower garden, 65% of the flowers are tulips. What fraction of Miranda's flowers are tulips?

A. $\frac{100}{65}$ C. $\frac{65}{1}$

B. $\frac{13}{20}$ D. $\frac{7}{40}$

FREE RESPONSE

12. Use the tables to compare the ratios $\frac{7}{8}$ and $\frac{11}{12}$.

7				
8				

11				
12				

$\frac{7}{8}$ ▢ $\frac{11}{12}$

13. Paula's dog, Toby, weighs 95 pounds.

Weight/Mass
1 pound ≈ 0.454 kilogram

a. To find Toby's weight in kilograms, what conversion factor should you use?

_____

b. Explain why multiplying a quantity by a conversion factor does not change the quantity's value.

_____

_____

_____

c. Find Toby's weight in kilograms.

_____

14. Samantha correctly answered 38 out of 55 questions on a test. She must score 70% or greater to pass the test. Did she pass? Justify your answer.

_____

_____

15. To earn money, Peter shovels driveways in the winter. He earns $24 in 3 hours.

a. Complete the table.

Hours	0.5	1	3	4	5
Amount Earned ($)			24		

b. Write the information in the table as ordered pairs. Use Hours as the x-coordinates and Amount earned as the y-coordinates.

_____

c. Graph the ordered pairs from **b** and connect the points.

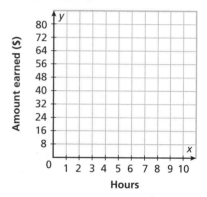

d. What is Peter's unit rate in dollars per hour? How are the table and the graph above related to this unit rate?

_____

_____

_____

e. How can you use the graph to find the amount of money Peter earns in 6 hours?

_____

_____

_____

f. How can you use the unit rate to find the amount of money Peter earns in 6 hours?

_____

Geometry

Unit Focus

In this unit you will learn about two- and three-dimensional figures. You will learn how to find the areas of polygons like triangles and quadrilaterals. You will find the volume of a prism. You will use nets to find surface area. You will apply all of these measurements in both real-world and mathematical situations.

Unit at a Glance

COMMON CORE

Lesson		Standards for Mathematical Content
6-1	Area of Triangles	CC.6.G.1
6-2	Area of Quadrilaterals	CC.6.G.1
6-3	Area of Polygons	CC.6.G.1
6-4	Polygons in the Coordinate Plane	CC.6.G.3
6-5	Volume of Prisms	CC.6.G.2
6-6	Nets and Surface Area	CC.6.G.4
	Problem Solving Connections	
	Test Prep	

UNIT 6

Unpacking the Common Core State Standards

Use the table to help you understand the Standards for Mathematical Content that are taught in this unit. Refer to the lessons listed after each standard for exploration and practice.

COMMON CORE Standards for Mathematical Content	What It Means For You
CC.6.G.1 Find the area of right triangles, other triangles, …; apply these techniques in the context of solving real-world and mathematical problems. Lesson 6-1	You will find the areas of triangles to solve both real-world and mathematical problems.
CC.6.G.1 Find the area of … special quadrilaterals, …; apply these techniques in the context of solving real-world and mathematical problems. Lesson 6-2	You will find the areas of special quadrilaterals to solve both real-world and mathematical problems.
CC.6.G.1 Find the area of … polygons by composing into rectangles or decomposing into triangles and other shapes; apply these techniques in the context of solving real-world and mathematical problems. Lesson 6-3	You will learn a variety of methods to find the areas of polygons to solve both real-world and mathematical problems.
CC.6.G.3 Draw polygons in the coordinate plane given coordinates for the vertices; use coordinates to find the length of a side joining points with the same first coordinate or the same second coordinate. Apply these techniques in the context of solving real-world or mathematical problems. Lesson 6-4	You will graph polygons in the coordinate plane, given coordinates for the vertices. You will use coordinates to find the length of a polygon's side.
CC.6.G.2 Find the volume of a right rectangular prism with fractional edge lengths by packing it with unit cubes of the appropriate unit fraction edge lengths, and show that the volume is the same as would be found by multiplying the edge lengths of the prism. Apply the formulas $V = lwh$ and $V = bh$ to find volumes of right rectangular prisms with fractional edge lengths in the context of solving real-world and mathematical problems. Lesson 6-5	You will find the volume of a right rectangular prism with fractional edge lengths to solve both real-world and mathematical problems.
CC.6.G.4 Represent three-dimensional figures using nets made up of rectangles and triangles, and use these nets to find the surface area of these figures. Apply these techniques in the context of solving real-world and mathematical problems. Lesson 6-6	You will use nets to find the surface area of three-dimensional figures and use this technique to solve real-world and mathematical problems.

UNIT 6

Area of Triangles

Essential question: *How do you find the area of a triangle?*

COMMON
CORE

CC.6.G.1

1 EXPLORE Area of a Right Triangle

A Draw a large rectangle on grid paper.

What is the formula for the area of a rectangle? $A =$ _____

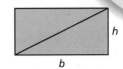

B Draw one diagonal of your rectangle.

The diagonal divides the rectangle into _____.
Each one represents _____ of the rectangle.

Use this information and the formula for area of a rectangle to

write a formula for the area of a right triangle. $A =$ _____

REFLECT

1. In the formula for the area of a right triangle, what do b and h represent?

_____

2 EXPLORE Area of a Triangle

A Draw a large triangle on grid paper. Do not draw a right triangle.

B Cut out your triangle. Then trace around it to make a copy of your triangle.
Cut out the copy.

C Cut one of your triangles into two pieces by cutting through
one angle directly across to the opposite side. Now you have
three triangles — one large triangle and two smaller triangles.

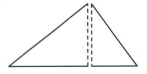

When added together, the areas of the two smaller triangles
equal the _____ of the large triangle.

D Arrange the three triangles into a rectangle. What fraction

of the rectangle does the large triangle represent? _____

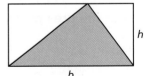

The area of the rectangle is $A = bh$. What is the area of

the large triangle? $A =$ _____

How does this formula compare to the formula for the area of a
right triangle that you found in **1** ?

_____

2. In the formula for the area of a triangle, what do b and h represent?

_____

_____

Area of a Triangle

$A = \frac{1}{2}bh$

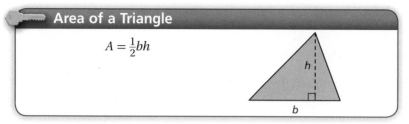

3 **EXAMPLE** **Finding the Area of a Triangle**

Find the area of each triangle.

A

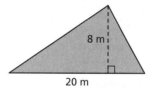

8 m
20 m

$b =$ _____ meters

$h =$ _____ meters

Use the formula to find the area. $A = \frac{1}{2}bh$

$= \frac{1}{2} \left(\boxed{} \text{ meters} \right) \left(\boxed{} \text{ meters} \right)$

$= \boxed{}$ square meters

B

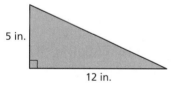

5 in.
12 in.

$b =$ _____ inches

$h =$ _____ inches

Use the formula to find the area. $A = \frac{1}{2}bh$

$= \frac{1}{2} \left(\boxed{} \text{ inches} \right) \left(\boxed{} \text{ inches} \right)$

$= \boxed{}$ square inches

TRY THIS!

Find the area of each triangle.

3a.

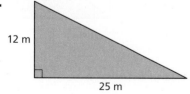

12 m
25 m

3b.

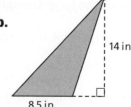

14 in.
8.5 in.

$A =$ _____

$A =$ _____

4 EXAMPLE   Problem Solving Using Areas of Triangles

The Hudson High School wrestling team just won the state tournament and has been awarded a triangular pennant to hang on the wall in the school gymnasium. What is the area of the pennant?

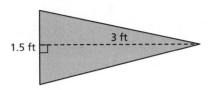

$b = $ _____ feet

$h = $ _____ feet

Use the formula to find the area.

$$A = \frac{1}{2}bh$$

$$= \frac{1}{2}\left(\boxed{} \text{ feet}\right)\left(\boxed{} \text{ feet}\right)$$

$$= \boxed{} \text{ square feet}$$

TRY THIS!

4a. Renee is sewing a quilt whose pattern contains right triangles. What is the area of one triangular quilt piece?

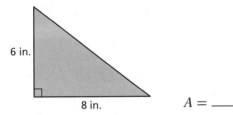

$A = $ _____

4b. William is making a model of a dinosaur. The dinosaur has triangular plates along its back. What is the area of each model plate?

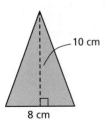

$A = $ _____

REFLECT

4c. When can you use two side lengths to find the area of a triangle? In this situation, does it matter which side is the base and which side is the height?

_____

_____

Find the area of each triangle.

1.

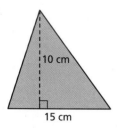

10 cm

15 cm

$A =$ _____

2.

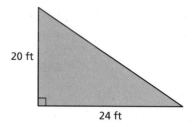

20 ft

24 ft

$A =$ _____

3.

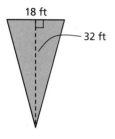

18 ft

32 ft

$A =$ _____

4.

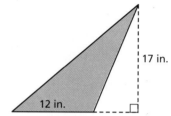

17 in.

12 in.

$A =$ _____

5. $b = 8\frac{1}{2}$ inches; $h = 15$ inches

$A =$ _____

6. $b = 15\frac{1}{4}$ inches; $h = 18$ inches

$A =$ _____

7. $b = 132$ meters; $h = 72$ meters

$A =$ _____

8. $b = 44$ feet; $h = 48$ feet

$A =$ _____

9. What is the area of the triangular plot of land?

$A =$ _____

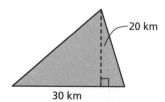

20 km

30 km

10. The sixth grade art students are making a mosaic using tiles in the shape of right triangles. Each tile has leg measures 3 centimeters and 5 centimeters. What is the area of one tile? $A =$ _____

11. A triangular piece of fabric has an area of 45 square inches. The height of the triangle is 15 inches. What is the length of the triangle's base?

$b =$ _____

12. The front part of a tent is 8 feet wide and 5 feet tall. What is the area of this part of the tent? $A =$ _____

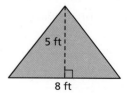

5 ft

8 ft

Area of Quadrilaterals

Essential question: *How can you find the areas of parallelograms, rhombuses, and trapezoids?*

COMMON
CORE

CC.6.G.1

1 EXPLORE   Area of a Parallelogram

A   Draw a large parallelogram on grid paper. Cut out your parallelogram.

B   Cut your parallelogram on the dashed line as shown. Then move the triangular piece to the other side of the parallelogram.

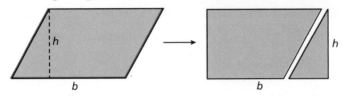

C   What figure have you formed? _____

     Does this figure have the same area as the parallelogram? _____

     What is the formula for the area of this figure? $A =$ _____

D   What is the formula for the area of a parallelogram? $A =$ _____

TRY THIS!

Find the area of each parallelogram.

1a.

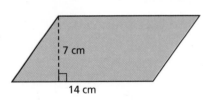

1b.

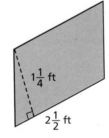

$A =$ _____ $A =$ _____

REFLECT

1c.   Why is the formula for the area of a parallelogram the same as the formula for the area of a rectangle?

_____

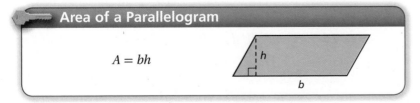

Area of a Parallelogram

$A = bh$

A **rhombus** is a quadrilateral in which all sides are congruent and opposite sides are parallel. A rhombus can be divided into four triangles that can then be rearranged into a rectangle.

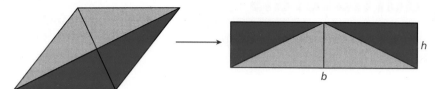

The base of the rectangle is the same length as one of the diagonals of the rhombus. The height of the rectangle is $\frac{1}{2}$ the length of the other diagonal.

$$A = b \cdot h$$
$$\downarrow \qquad \downarrow$$
$$A = d_1 \cdot \frac{1}{2} d_2$$

Area of a Rhombus

$$A = \frac{1}{2} d_1 d_2$$

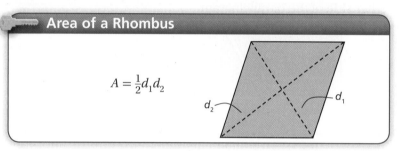

2 EXAMPLE   Finding the Area of a Rhombus

Cedric is constructing a kite in the shape of a rhombus. The spars of the kite measure 15 inches and 24 inches. How much fabric will Cedric need for the kite?

To determine the amount of fabric needed, find the area of the kite.

$d_1 = $ _____ $d_2 = $ _____

Use the formula for area of a rhombus.

$A = \frac{1}{2} d_1 d_2$

$= \frac{1}{2} \left(\quad \right) \left(\quad \right)$

$= \boxed{}$ square inches

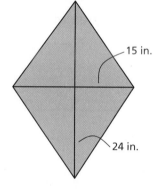

15 in.

24 in.

TRY THIS!

Find the area of each rhombus.

2a. $d_1 = 35$ m; $d_2 = 12$ m

$A = $ _____ m^2

2b. $d_1 = 9.5$ in.; $d_2 = 14$ in.

$A = $ _____ in^2

2c. $d_1 = 10$ m; $d_2 = 18$ m

$A = $ _____ m^2

2d. $d_1 = 8\frac{1}{4}$ ft; $d_2 = 40$ ft

$A = $ _____ ft^2

To find the formula for the area of a trapezoid, notice that two copies of the same trapezoid fit together to form a parallelogram. Therefore, the area of the trapezoid is $\frac{1}{2}$ the area of the parallelogram.

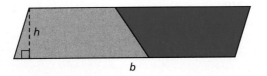

The height of the parallelogram is the same as the height of the trapezoid. The base of the parallelogram is the sum of the two bases of the trapezoid.

$$A = \quad b \quad \cdot h$$
$$\downarrow$$
$$A = \overbrace{(b_1 + b_2)} \cdot h$$

$$A = \tfrac{1}{2}h(b_1 + b_2)$$

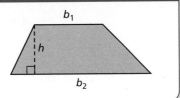

3 EXAMPLE   Finding the Area of a Trapezoid

A section of a deck is in the shape of a trapezoid. What is the area of this section of the deck?

$b_1 = $ _____ $b_2 = $ _____ $h = $ _____

Use the formula for area of a trapezoid.

$A = \frac{1}{2}h(b_1 + b_2)$

$= \frac{1}{2} \cdot \boxed{} \left(\boxed{} + \boxed{} \right)$

$= \frac{1}{2} \cdot \boxed{} \left(\boxed{} \right)$ *Add inside the parentheses.*

$= 8 \cdot \boxed{}$ *Multiply $\frac{1}{2}$ and 16.*

$= \boxed{}$ square feet   *Multiply.*

17 ft

16 ft

39 ft

TRY THIS!

3a. Another section of the deck is also shaped as a trapezoid. For this section, the length of one base is 27 feet, and the length of the other base is 34 feet. The height is 12 feet. What is the area of this section of the deck? $A = $ _____ ft^2

REFLECT

3b. Does it matter which of the trapezoid's bases is substituted for b_1 and which is substituted for b_2? Why or why not?

_____

_____

Find the area of each parallelogram.

1.

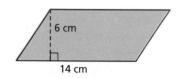

$A =$ _____ cm^2

2.

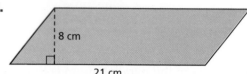

$A =$ _____ cm^2

3. $b = 13$ meters; $h = 7$ meters

$A =$ _____ m^2

4. $b = 12\frac{3}{4}$ inches; $h = 2\frac{1}{2}$ inches

$A =$ _____ in^2

Find the area of each rhombus.

5.

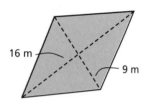

$A =$ _____ m^2

6.

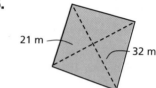

$A =$ _____ m^2

7. $d_1 = 18$ feet; $d_2 = 7.25$ feet

$A =$ _____ ft^2

8. $d_1 = 8$ inches; $d_2 = 2\frac{1}{2}$ inches

$A =$ _____ in^2

Find the area of each trapezoid.

9.

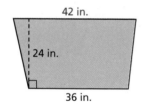

$A =$ _____ in^2

10.

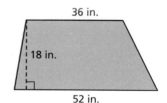

$A =$ _____ in^2

11. $b_1 = 9$ meters
$b_2 = 15$ meters
$h = 8$ meters

$A =$ _____ m^2

12. $b_1 = 11$ meters
$b_2 = 14$ meters
$h = 10$ meters

$A =$ _____ m^2

13. Find the area of the figure. Explain how you found your answer.

_____

_____

_____

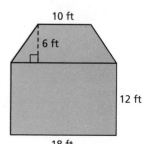

Name _____ Class _____ Date _____

Area of Polygons

Essential question: *How can you find the area of a polygon by breaking it into simpler shapes?*

COMMON CORE

CC.6.G.1

---

1 EXPLORE   Area Using Tangrams

The area of the small square is 1 square unit. Find the area of each of the other tangram pieces.

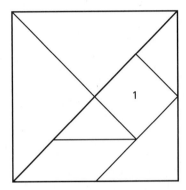

A Place one large triangle on top of the other large triangle. What is true about these two triangles? What does this mean about the areas of these two triangles?

_____

B What is true about the areas of the two small triangles?

_____

C Place the two small triangles on top of the square. Remember that the area of

the square is 1. What is the area of each small triangle? _____ Write this area on the diagram.

D Arrange the square and one of the small triangles as shown.

What is the combined area? _____

Now place the parallelogram and the other small triangle on top of the combined square and triangle. What is true about the combined area of the parallelogram and one small triangle?

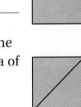

_____

The two small triangles have _____ area. Therefore, the area of the parallelogram is the same as the area of the _____.

Write the area of the parallelogram on the diagram.

1. Complete the rest of the diagram by filling in the remaining areas. Explain how you found your answers.

_____

_____

_____

2 EXAMPLE Finding the Area of a Polygon

Find the area of each polygon.

A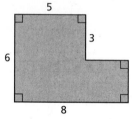

Step 1 Draw a horizontal line segment on the diagram that divides the polygon into two rectangles, one on top of the other.

What is the length of this segment? _____ Label this length on the diagram.

Step 2 Find the area of the smaller (top) rectangle.

$A = bh =$ ☐ · ☐ = ☐ square units

Step 3 Find the area of the larger (bottom) rectangle.

The base of the larger rectangle is _____.

The height is 6 − ☐ = ☐.

$A = bh =$ ☐ · ☐ = ☐ square units

Step 4 Add the areas from Steps 2 and 3 to find the total area.

$A =$ ☐ + ☐ = ☐ square units

REFLECT

2a. Redraw the original polygon. Divide the polygon into two rectangles in a different way and use these two rectangles to find the area.

2b. Does the way you divide the original polygon affect the final answer? _____

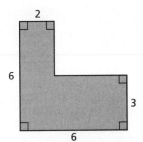

Step 1 On the diagram, form a square with a "missing piece": Extend the top side of the polygon to the right and extend the right side of the polygon up.

What is the side length of this square? _____

The area of the square is ▢ • ▢ = ▢ square units.

Step 2 Find the area of the rectangular "missing piece".

$b = 6 - 2 =$ ▢ $h = 6 -$ ▢ $=$ ▢

$A = bh =$ ▢ • ▢ $=$ ▢ square units

Step 3 Subtract the area in Step 2 from the area in Step 1.

$A =$ ▢ $-$ ▢ $=$ ▢ square units

C

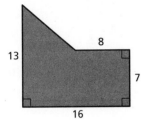

Step 1 Draw a horizontal line segment on the diagram that divides the polygon into a rectangle and a triangle.

Step 2 Find the area of the rectangle.

$A = bh =$ ▢ • ▢ $=$ ▢ square units

Step 3 Find the area of the triangle.

$b = 16 -$ ▢ $=$ ▢ $h = 13 -$ ▢ $=$ ▢

$A = \frac{1}{2}bh = \frac{1}{2} \cdot$ ▢ • ▢ $=$ ▢ square units

Step 4 Add the areas from Steps 2 and 3 to find the total area.

$A =$ ▢ $+$ ▢ $=$ ▢ square units

TRY THIS!

Find the area of each polygon.

2c.

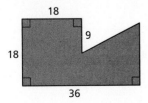

$A =$ _____ square units

2d.

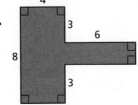

$A =$ _____ square units

Find the area of each polygon.

1.

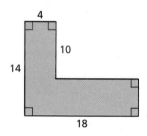

$A =$ _____ square units

2.

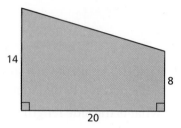

$A =$ _____ square units

3.

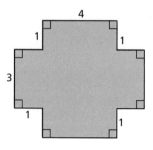

$A =$ _____ square units

4.

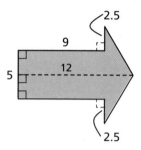

$A =$ _____ square units

5. In Hal's backyard, there is a patio, a walkway, and a garden.

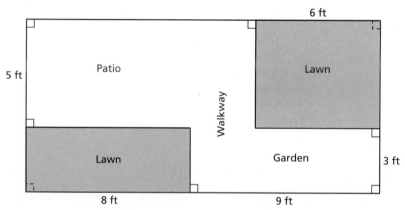

a. Show how to find the total area of the patio, walkway, and garden by adding areas of rectangles.

b. Show how to find the total area of the patio, walkway, and garden by subtracting areas of rectangles.

Polygons in the Coordinate Plane

COMMON
CORE

CC.6.G.3

Essential question: *How can you solve problems by drawing polygons in the coordinate plane?*

A **vertex** is a point common to two sides of an angle, a polygon, or a three-dimensional figure. The *vertices* of a polygon can be represented by ordered pairs, and the polygon can then be drawn in the coordinate plane.

---

1 **EXPLORE** Polygons in the Coordinate Plane

A clothing designer makes letters for varsity jackets by graphing the letters as polygons on a coordinate plane. One of the letters is polygon *ABCDEF* with the following vertices.

$A(3, -2)$, $B(3, -4)$, $C(-3, -4)$, $D(-3, 4)$,
$E(-1, 4)$, $F(-1, -2)$

Graph the points on the coordinate plane and connect them in order.

What letter is formed? _____

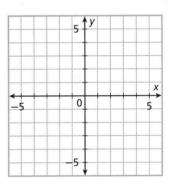

Polygons are named by the number of their sides and angles. A **regular polygon** is a polygon in which all sides have the same length and all angles have the same measure.

Polygon	Sides and Angles	Regular	Not Regular
Triangle	3		
Quadrilateral	4		
Pentagon	5		
Hexagon	6		
Heptagon	7		
Octagon	8		

2 EXAMPLE · Finding Perimeter in the Coordinate Plane

This afternoon, Tommy walked from his home to the library. He then walked to the park. From the park, he visited a friend's house, and the two of them walked to a nearby goldfish pond. Tommy left the goldfish pond and stopped at the store before returning home.

A The coordinates of each location are given. Graph and connect the points to show Tommy's path.

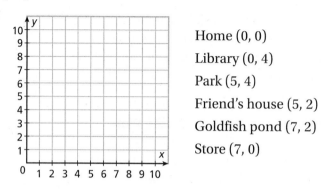

Home (0, 0)

Library (0, 4)

Park (5, 4)

Friend's house (5, 2)

Goldfish pond (7, 2)

Store (7, 0)

B Each grid unit represents one block. What is the distance from Tommy's home to the library?

You can use coordinates to find the distance between two points.

If two points have the same x-coordinate, find the distance by subtracting the y-coordinates.

The distance from Tommy's home at (0, 0) to the library at (0, 4) is $4 - 0 = $ ▢ blocks.

C What is the distance from Tommy's friend's house to the goldfish pond?

If two points have the same y-coordinate, find the distance by subtracting the x-coordinates.

The distance from Tommy's friend's house at (5, 2) to the goldfish pond at (7, 2) is ▢ $-$ ▢ $=$ ▢ blocks.

TRY THIS!

2a. What does the perimeter of the polygon represent?

_____

2b. Calculate the remaining distances. Then find the perimeter.

Library to park _____ blocks   Park to friend's house _____ blocks

Goldfish pond to store _____ blocks   Store to home _____ blocks

Perimeter = _____ blocks

The polygon shown is a regular polygon. Use this polygon to answer the following questions.

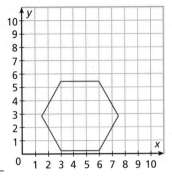

2c. How many sides does the polygon have? _____
This polygon is a regular _____ .

2d. What is the length of each side? _____ units. How do you know?

_____

_____

2e. Use your answer to **2d** to find the perimeter.

_____

3 EXAMPLE Finding Area in the Coordinate Plane

John is planning a new deck for his house. He has graphed the deck as polygon *ABCDEF* on a coordinate plane in which each grid unit represents one foot. The vertices of this polygon are $A(1, 0)$, $B(3, 2)$, $C(3, 5)$, $D(8, 5)$, $E(8, 2)$, and $F(6, 0)$. What is the area of John's deck?

Step 1 Graph the vertices and connect them in order.

Draw a horizontal dashed line segment to divide the polygon into two quadrilaterals—a rectangle and a parallelogram.

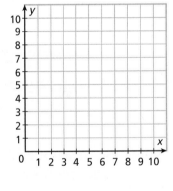

Step 2 Find the area of the rectangle.

$b =$ _____ feet $h =$ _____ feet

$A = bh =$ ☐ · ☐ = ☐ square feet

Step 3 Find the area of the parallelogram.

$b =$ _____ feet $h =$ _____ feet

$A = bh =$ ☐ · ☐ = ☐ square feet

Step 4 Add the areas from Steps 2 and 3 to find the total area of the deck.

$A =$ ☐ + ☐ = ☐ square feet

TRY THIS!

3. Tabitha is making a wall hanging. She has graphed the wall hanging as polygon *LMNOPQ* on a coordinate plane. The vertices of this polygon are $L(1, 2)$, $M(1, 6)$, $N(7, 6)$, $O(7, 2)$, $P(5, 0)$, and $Q(3, 0)$. Graph the polygon on the coordinate plane. What is the area of Tabitha's wall hanging?

$A =$ _____ square units

PRACTICE

Give the name of each polygon.

1.

_____

2.

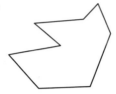

_____

3.

_____

4.

_____

5. A clothing designer makes letters for varsity jackets by graphing the letters as polygons on a coordinate plane. One of the letters is polygon *MNOPQRSTUV* with vertices *M*(2, 1), *N*(2, 9), *O*(7, 9), *P*(7, 7), *Q*(4, 7), *R*(4, 6), *S*(6, 6), *T*(6, 4), *U*(4, 4), and *V*(4, 1).

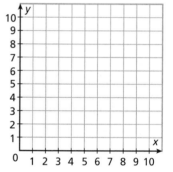

    a. Graph the points on the coordinate plane and connect them in order.

    b. What letter is formed? _____

    c. Find the perimeter and area.

        P = _____ units   *A* = _____ square units

Give the name of each polygon. Then find its perimeter and area. Some side lengths are given.

6.

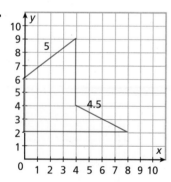

_____

    P = _____ units

    A = _____ square units

7.

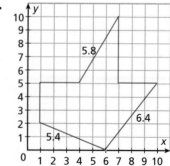

_____

    P = _____ units

    A = _____ square units

Volume of Prisms

Essential question: *How do you find the volume of a rectangular prism?*

COMMON CORE

CC.6.G.2

1 EXPLORE Volume of a Prism

A cube with edge length 1 unit and volume 1 cubic unit is
filled with smaller cubes as shown.

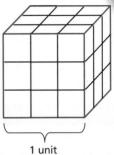

1 unit

A How many small cubes are there? _____

How does the combined volume of the small cubes
compare to the volume of the large cube?

_____

Number of small cubes	·	Volume of one small cube	=	Volume of large cube

 · **?** =

What is the volume of one small cube? _____ cubic unit(s)

B Each edge of the large cube contains _____ small cubes.

Number of small cubes per edge	·	Edge length of one small cube	=	Edge length of large cube

 · **?** =

What is the edge length of one small cube? _____ unit(s)

C Combine your results from **A** and **B** to complete the following sentence.

Each small cube has edge length _____ unit(s) and volume _____ cubic unit(s).

D Remember that the formula for volume of a cube with edge length ℓ is
$V = \ell \cdot \ell \cdot \ell$, or $V = \ell^3$.

Show how to find the volume of one small cube using this formula.

$V = $ _____ = _____

E Several of the small cubes are arranged into a medium-sized cube as shown.

Show two different ways to find the volume of the medium-sized cube.

Volume of a Rectangular Prism

$V = \ell wh$, or $V = Bh$
(where B represents the area of
the prism's base; $B = \ell w$.)

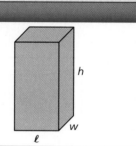

---

2 **EXAMPLE** **Finding Volume**

Find the volume of the rectangular prism.

$\ell =$ _____ meters $w =$ _____ meters $h =$ _____ meters

$V = \ell\,wh$

= ☐ · ☐ · ☐

= ☐ · ☐ · ☐   *Write each mixed number as an improper fraction.*

= ☐   *Multiply.*

= ☐   cubic meters   *Write as a mixed number in simplest form.*

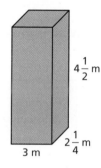

4½ m

2¼ m

3 m

REFLECT

2a. Show how to use the formula $V = Bh$ to find the volume.

TRY THIS!

Find the volume of each rectangular prism.

2b.

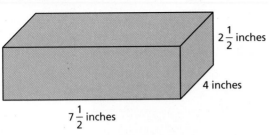

$2\frac{1}{2}$ inches

4 inches

$7\frac{1}{2}$ inches

$V =$ _____ cubic inches

2c. length $= 5\frac{1}{4}$ inches

width $= 3\frac{1}{2}$ inches

height $= 3$ inches

$V =$ _____ cubic inches

---

3 **EXAMPLE** **Problem-Solving by Finding Volume**

A rectangular city swimming pool is 25 meters long, $17\frac{1}{2}$ meters wide, and has an average depth of $1\frac{1}{2}$ meters. What is the volume of the pool?

Label the rectangular prism to represent the pool.

$\ell =$ _____ meters $w =$ _____ meters $h =$ _____ meters

$V = \ell w h$

$= $ ▢ · ▢ · ▢

$= $ ▢ · ▢ · ▢   *Write each mixed number as an*
                                improper fraction.

$= $ ▢   *Multiply.*

$= $ ▢ cubic meters   *Write as a mixed number in simplest form.*

TRY THIS!

3a. Miguel has a turtle aquarium that measures $18\frac{1}{2}$ inches by $12\frac{1}{2}$ inches by 4 inches. What is the volume of the aquarium?

$V =$ _____ cubic inches

REFLECT

3b. How can you use estimation to check the reasonableness of your answer to **3a**?

_____

_____

Find the volume of each rectangular prism.

1.

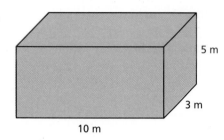

5 m
3 m
10 m

$V =$ _____ cubic meters

2.

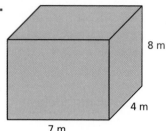

8 m
4 m
7 m

$V =$ _____ cubic meters

3.

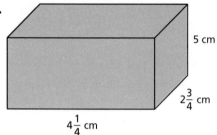

5 cm
$2\frac{3}{4}$ cm
$4\frac{1}{4}$ cm

$V =$ _____ cubic centimeters

4.

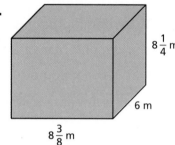

$8\frac{1}{4}$ m
6 m
$8\frac{3}{8}$ m

$V =$ _____ cubic meters

5.

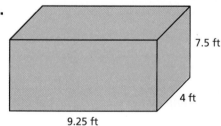

7.5 ft
4 ft
9.25 ft

$V =$ _____ cubic feet

6.

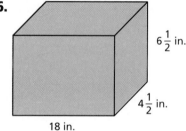

$6\frac{1}{2}$ in.
$4\frac{1}{2}$ in.
18 in.

$V =$ _____ cubic inches

7. A block of wood measures 4.5 centimeters by 3.5 centimeters by 7 centimeters. What is the volume of the block of wood?

$V =$ _____ cubic centimeters

8. A restaurant buys a freezer in the shape of a rectangular prism. The dimensions of the freezer are shown. What is the volume of the freezer?

$V =$ _____ cubic inches

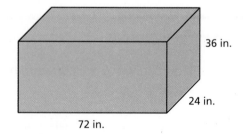

36 in.
24 in.
72 in.

9. Conjecture The length, width, and height of a rectangular prism are doubled. How many times greater is the volume compared to the original prism?

Nets and Surface Area

COMMON
CORE

CC.6.G.4

Essential question: *How can you use nets to find surface areas?*

A **net** is a two-dimensional pattern of shapes that can be folded into a three-dimensional figure. The shapes in the net become the faces of the three-dimensional figure.

1 EXPLORE   Nets of a Cube

A Copy the following nets on graph paper and cut them out along the blue lines.

Net A

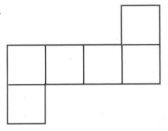

Net B

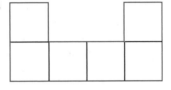

One of these nets can be folded along the black lines to make a cube. Which net will NOT make a cube? _____

B See if you can find another net that can be folded into a cube.

Draw a net that you think will make a cube on your graph paper, and then cut it out. Can you fold it into a cube?

C Compare your results with several of your classmates. How many different nets for a cube did you and your classmates find?

_____

REFLECT

How do you know that each net cannot be folded into a cube without actually cutting and folding it?

1a.

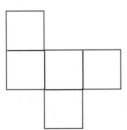

1b.

_____   _____

_____   _____

1c. What shapes will appear in a net for a rectangular prism that is not a cube? How many of these shapes will there be?

_____

The **surface area** of a three-dimensional figure is the sum of the areas of its faces. A net can be helpful when finding surface area.

2 EXPLORE Surface Area of a Rectangular Prism

The gift wrap department of a store has specially sized boxes to wrap sweaters. Use the box's dimensions to label the dimensions of the net. Then find the surface area of the box.

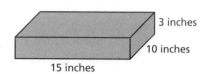

3 inches
10 inches
15 inches

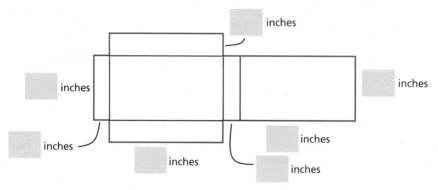

inches

inches

inches

inches

inches

inches

inches

Complete the table to find the surface area.

Face	Base (in.)	Height (in.)	Area (in²)
Top	15	10	150
Bottom			
Front			
Back			
Right			
Left			
		Total	

The surface area of the sweater box is _____ square inches.

REFLECT

2a. How did you find the area of each face?

_____

2b. If the box had been a cube, how would finding the surface area have been easier?

_____

_____

A **pyramid** is a three-dimensional figure whose base is a polygon and whose other faces are all triangles. A pyramid is named by its base. A pyramid whose base is a triangle is a triangular pyramid. A pyramid whose base is a square is a square pyramid, and so on.

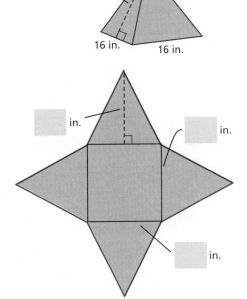

3 EXPLORE   Surface Area of a Pyramid

Find the surface area of the pyramid.

17 in.

16 in.   16 in.

A   How many faces does the pyramid have? _____

B   What polygon forms the base of the pyramid?

_____

What is the formula for the area of this polygon?

$A =$ _____

C   What polygon forms each of the other faces? What is the formula for the area of this polygon?

_____

D   Complete the net by labeling its dimensions.

E   Complete the table to find the surface area.

Face	Base (in.)	Height (in.)	Area (in²)
Base	16		
Triangle			
Triangle			
Triangle			
Triangle			
		Total	

The surface area of the pyramid is _____ square inches.

REFLECT

3a. What would have been a quicker way to find the combined areas of the triangles?

_____

3b. Surface area is measured in square units. Why are square units used when working with a three-dimensional figure?

_____

PRACTICE

Identify the three-dimensional figure formed by each net.

1.

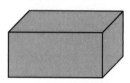

_____

2.

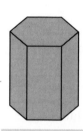

_____

Draw a net for each three-dimensional figure.

3.

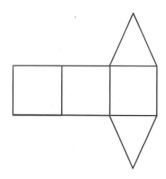

4.

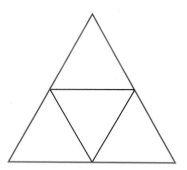

Find the surface area of each figure.

5.

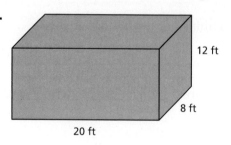

12 ft

8 ft

20 ft

_____ square feet

6.

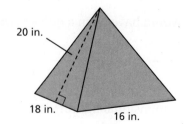

20 in.

18 in.

16 in.

_____ square inches

UNIT 6

COMMON CORE

CC.6.G.1
CC.6.G.2
CC.6.G.3
CC.6.G.4

Problem Solving Connections

Something's Fishy As a birthday surprise for their son Wyatt, Mr. and Mrs. Watson plan to purchase a large aquarium, its accessories, and all of Wyatt's favorite species of tropical fish. Once they have decided on an aquarium, Mr. Watson will build a stand for it, and then they will decide how many fish to buy.

1 Volume

After looking at several different aquariums, Mr. and Mrs. Watson have decided to purchase either tank A or tank B.

A Find the volume of tank A.

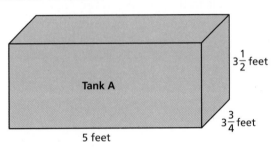

Tank A

$3\frac{1}{2}$ feet

$3\frac{3}{4}$ feet

5 feet

B Find the volume of tank B.

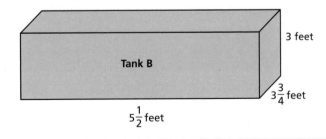

Tank B

3 feet

$3\frac{3}{4}$ feet

$5\frac{1}{2}$ feet

C The Watsons decide to purchase the tank with the greater volume. Which tank is this? How much greater is its volume than that of the other tank?

D A box of fish food is 2.25 inches long, 1.5 inches wide, and 4 inches tall. What is the volume of the box of fish food?

E The filter system for the aquarium is in the shape of a rectangular prism. It measures $8\frac{1}{2}$ inches long, $8\frac{1}{2}$ inches wide, and 15 inches high. What is the volume of filter system?

2 Surface Area

Mrs. Watson is wrapping the accessories for the aquarium. She will find the surface area of each box to determine how much gift wrap she needs.

Aquarium Light Kit

3 in.

7.5 in.

2 in.

A Find the surface area of the box for the light kit.

B Find the surface area of the box for the heater.

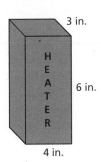

3 in.

HEATER

6 in.

4 in.

3 Area and Perimeter

A A rectangular backdrop for the aquarium measures 5 feet by 3.5 feet. What is the area that the back drop will cover?

B Mr. Watson has a solid rectangular piece of birch plywood for the top of the aquarium stand. The plywood is 6 feet long and $4\frac{3}{4}$ feet wide. He plans to attach decorative trim around the front and side edges. How much trim does he need?

C Mr. Watson removes a rectangle from the top back edge of the stand, as shown, to allow space for electrical cords. Will the aquarium still fit on the stand in front of this space? Explain.

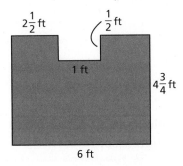

$2\frac{1}{2}$ ft $\frac{1}{2}$ ft

1 ft

$4\frac{3}{4}$ ft

6 ft

D What is the area of the top of the stand? Explain how you found your answer.

E Find the area of the top of the stand using a different method than the one you used in **D** .

4 Answer the Question

A One gallon of water fills 231 cubic inches of space. About how many gallons of water are needed to fill the aquarium? (*Hint*: There are 1,728 cubic inches in a cubic foot.)

B It is recommended that there be at least 12 gallons of water in the aquarium for each fish. Using this rule, what is the maximum number of fish the Watsons should purchase for the aquarium?

C If the Watsons had purchased the smaller tank, what would be the maximum number of fish they should purchase?

Name _____ Class _____ Date _____

MULTIPLE CHOICE

1. New tiles are being laid in the school hallway. The tiles measure 1 foot by 1 foot. The hallway is 75 feet long and 9 feet wide. How many tiles will be needed to cover the floor of the hallway?

   A. 84 tiles   C. 675 tiles

   B. 168 tiles   D. 6,075 tiles

2. A triangular street sign has a base of 30 inches and a height of 24 inches.

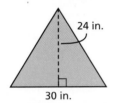

   What is the area of the street sign?

   F. 54 square inches

   G. 114 square inches

   H. 360 square inches

   J. 720 square inches

3. Martha is putting a wallpaper border along the tops of the four walls in her bedroom. The room is a rectangle that measures 12 feet by 10 feet. One package of wallpaper border is 9 feet long. How many packages does Martha need?

   A. 2 packages   C. 5 packages

   B. 4 packages   D. 14 packages

4. A regular polygon has a perimeter of 48 feet. Each side of the polygon measures 6 feet. What is the name of this polygon?

   F. triangle   H. hexagon

   G. square   J. octagon

5. A triangular pennant has a base of 12 inches and a height of 18 inches. What is the area of the pennant?

   A. 30 square inches

   B. 66 square inches

   C. 108 square inches

   D. 216 square inches

6. Which statement about the square and the rectangle is correct?

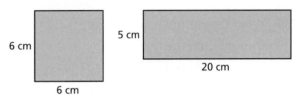

   F. They have the same perimeter and the same area.

   G. They have the same perimeter but different areas.

   H. They have different perimeters but the same area.

   J. They have different perimeters and different areas.

7. Katrina is making a wall hanging in the shape of a trapezoid.

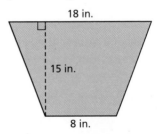

   What is the area of Katrina's wall hanging?

   A. 144 square inches

   B. 195 square inches

   C. 270 square inches

   D. 390 square inches

8. What is the area of the parallelogram?

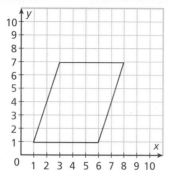

F. 24 square units

G. 30 square units

H. 35 square units

J. 42 square units

9. What three-dimensional figure will be formed from the net?

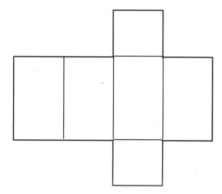

A. triangular prism

B. square pyramid

C. rectangular prism

D. triangular pyramid

10. What is the surface area of the rectangular prism?

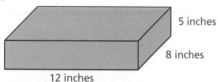

5 inches
8 inches
12 inches

F. 192 square inches

G. 272 square inches

H. 392 square inches

J. 480 square inches

FREE RESPONSE

11. The volume of a rectangular prism is 810 cubic centimeters. The length is 18 centimeters and the width is 9 centimeters. What is the height? Explain how you found your answer.

_____

_____

12. Which package has the greater volume? How much greater is the volume? Show your work.

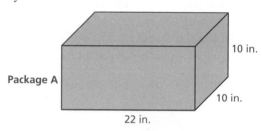

Package A

10 in.
10 in.
22 in.

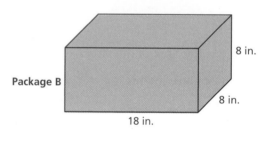

Package B

8 in.
8 in.
18 in.

_____

_____

_____

_____

13. Draw a net of a triangular pyramid.

Statistics

Unit Focus

In this unit, you will learn to identify statistical and non-statistical questions. You will draw dot plots and histograms to visually display data sets. Then you will calculate measures of center – the mean and median. You will also analyze the spread of data sets by drawing box plots, finding the interquartile range, and finding the mean absolute deviation.

Unit at a Glance

COMMON
CORE

UNIT 7

Unpacking the Common Core State Standards

Use the table to help you understand the Standards for Mathematical Content that are taught in this unit. Refer to the lessons listed after each standard for exploration and practice.

COMMON CORE Standards for Mathematical Content	What It Means For You
CC.6.SP.1 Recognize a statistical question as one that anticipates variability in the data related to the question and accounts for it in the answers. Lesson 7-1	You will identify statistical and non-statistical questions.
CC.6.SP.2 Understand that a set of data collected to answer a statistical question has a distribution which can be described by its center, spread, and overall shape. Lessons 7-1, 7-2, 7-3	You will display data in histograms, dot plots, and box plots; calculate the mean and median of a data set as measures of center; and find the interquartile range and mean absolute deviation of a data set.
CC.6.SP.3 Recognize that a measure of center for a numerical data set summarizes all of its values with a single number, while a measure of variation describes how its values vary with a single number. Lessons 7-2, 7-3	You will calculate mean and median and use them to describe a typical value of a data set. You will calculate interquartile range and mean absolute deviation to describe variability of a data set.
CC.6.SP.4 Display numerical data in ... dot plots, histograms, and box plots. Lessons 7-1, 7-3	You will display data in histograms, dot plots, and box plots.
CC.6.SP.5a Summarize numerical data sets in relation to their context, such as by: Reporting the number of observations. Lessons 7-1, 7-3	You will count the number of values in a data set.
CC.6.SP.5b Summarize numerical data sets in relation to their context, such as by: Describing the nature of the attribute under investigation, including how it was measured and its units of measurement. Lesson 7-1	You will identify the type of data measured and its unit of measurement.
CC.6.SP.5c Summarize numerical data sets in relation to their context, such as by: Giving quantitative measures of center (median and/or mean) and variability (interquartile range and/or mean absolute deviation), as well as describing any overall pattern and any striking deviations from the overall pattern with reference to the context in which the data were gathered. Lessons 7-2, 7-3	You will calculate mean, median, interquartile range, and mean absolute deviation for a data set.
CC.6.SP.5d Summarize numerical data sets in relation to their context, such as by: Relating the choice of measures of center and variability to the shape of the data distribution and the context in which the data were gathered. Lessons 7-2, 7-3	You will compare mean and median and use at least one of them to describe a typical value of a data set. You will compare interquartile range and mean absolute deviation and choose which one describes better the variability of the data set.

Displaying Numerical Data

Essential question: *How can you summarize and display numerical data?*

COMMON
CORE

CC.6.SP.1
CC.6.SP.2
CC.6.SP.4
CC.6.SP.5a
CC.6.SP.5b

Statistics is the process of collecting, organizing, and interpreting data. Statistics is used to plan and make future decisions and to answer *statistical questions*.

A **statistical question** is a question that has many different, or variable, answers.

1 EXPLORE Statistical Questions

Which of the following are statistical questions? Which are not?

- What is Mike's shoe size?
- What are the shoe sizes of students my age?
- How tall are my classmates?
- How tall is Joanie?
- How old is Chris's pet?
- How old are my friends' pets?
- How far does Terrence drive to work?
- How far do the employees of this store drive to work?

Statistical Questions	Non-Statistical Questions
_____	_____
_____	_____
_____	_____
_____	_____
_____	_____
_____	_____

REFLECT

1. Choose one of the statistical questions from **1** . How might you find the answers to this question? What units might the answers be in?

_____

_____

Statistical questions are answered by collecting and analyzing data. One way to understand a set of data is to make a visual display. A **dot plot** is a visual display in which each piece of data is represented by a dot above a number line.

2 EXAMPLE   Dot Plots

In games played during a two-week period, a baseball team scored the following numbers of runs:

$$12, 3, 8, 1, 1, 6, 10, 14, 3, 6, 2, 1, 3, 2, 7$$

Make a dot plot for the data.

How many games did the team play during this period? _____

What is the least number of runs scored? _____

What is the greatest number of runs scored? _____

Label the number line from the least number of runs to the greatest number of runs.

For each data value, draw a dot above the appropriate number. If a value repeats, draw a second dot directly above the previous dot.

Runs Scored

Runs

TRY THIS!

2a. In June 2010, opponents of the Boston Red Sox scored the following numbers of runs: 4, 4, 9, 0, 2, 4, 1, 2, 11, 8, 2, 2, 5, 3, 2, 5, 6, 4, 0. Make a dot plot for the data.

REFLECT

2b. How does a dot plot help you describe a data set? Use the dot plot in the Example or Try This to support your answer.

_____

_____

_____

_____

2c. The *frequency* of a data value is the number of times it occurs in a data set. How can you tell the frequency of a data value by looking at a dot plot?

_____

It is sometimes more convenient to show data that has been divided into intervals than to display individual data values. A **histogram** is a type of bar graph whose bars represent the frequencies of data within intervals.

3 EXAMPLE Histograms

Make a histogram for the data given in ② :
        12, 3, 8, 1, 1, 6, 10, 14, 3, 6, 2, 1, 3, 2, 7

Step 1 Make a frequency table.

Divide the data into equally-sized intervals of 4. Complete the frequency table.

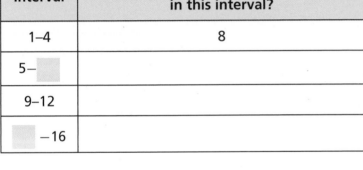

Interval	Frequency – How many data values are in this interval?
1–4	8
5–	
9–12	
–16	

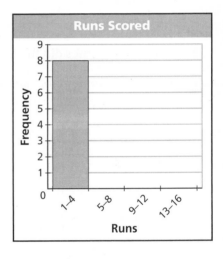

Step 2 Make a histogram.

The intervals are listed along the horizontal axis. For each interval, draw a bar to show the number of runs in that interval. The bars should have equal widths. They should touch but not overlap.

REFLECT

3. How is the histogram similar to the dot plot in ② ? How does it differ?

_____

_____

_____

_____

_____

_____

PRACTICE

Tell whether each question is statistical or non-statistical.

1. What are the incomes of your neighbors? _____

2. How old are the homes on your street? _____

3. What is your favorite movie? _____

The dot plot shows the number of runs scored by a baseball team in games played during the month of April. Use the dot plot for 4–9.

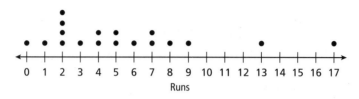

Runs Scored

4. What does each dot represent? _____

   _____

5. How many games did the team play in April? _____

6. Make a frequency table and histogram for the data.

Interval	Frequency
0–4	

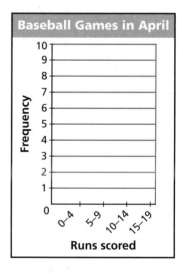

Baseball Games in April

7. What size are the intervals used to make the histogram? _____

8. Give an example of information provided by the dot plot that is not provided by the histogram.

   _____

   _____

9. The numbers of runs scored by the same team in games played during May are: 3, 5, 2, 5, 4, 7, 1, 0, 6, 4, 8, 5, 3, 2, 4, 5, 9. Add these data to the dot plot.

   Describe the shape of the data. Are there any data values that do not fit the overall shape? If so, which ones?

   _____

   _____

Measures of Center

Essential question: *How can you use measures of center to describe a data set?*

COMMON
CORE

CC.6.SP.2
CC.6.SP.3
CC.6.SP.5c
CC.6.SP.5d

A **measure of center** is a single number used to describe a data set. A measure of center describes a typical value from the data set.

One measure of center is the *mean*. The **mean**, or average, of a data set is the sum of the data values divided by the number of data values in the set.

1 EXPLORE Finding the Mean

Tami surveyed five of her friends to find out how many brothers and sisters they have. Her results are shown in the table.

Number of Siblings				
Amy	Ben	Cal	Don	Eva
2	3	1	1	3

A Model each person's response as a group of counters.

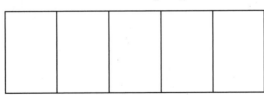

B Now rearrange the counters so that each group has the same number of counters.

Each group now has _____ counter(s). This value is the mean. This model demonstrates how the mean "evens out" the data values.

C Use numbers to calculate the mean.

The sum of the data values is 2 + 3 + ⬜ + ⬜ + ⬜ = ⬜.

How many data values are in the set? _____

$$\text{Mean} = \frac{\text{sum of data values}}{\text{number of data values}} = \frac{\boxed{}}{\boxed{}} = \boxed{}$$

TRY THIS!

1a. Find the mean of the data set: 10, 9, 4, 8, 8, 3, 6, 8. _____

1b. Suppose you have a data set in which all of the values are 2. What is the mean? _____

1c. Can the mean be greater than the greatest value in a data set? Why or why not?

_____

_____

_____

1d. The mean is **sometimes** / **always** / **never** a value in the data set.

Another measure of center is the *median*. The **median** represents the middle value of an ordered data set.

2 EXAMPLE   Finding the Median

A The distances that cross-country team members ran last week are shown. Find the median.

Distance Run (mi)
3 5 7 10 10 4
7 5 8 10 6

Write the data values in order from least to greatest.

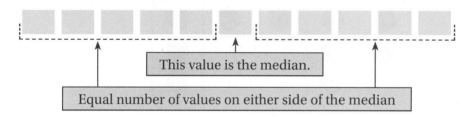

This value is the median.

Equal number of values on either side of the median

B The following are several student's test scores: 87, 90, 77, 83, 99, 94, 93, 90, 85, 83. Find the median.

Write the data values in order from least to greatest.

This data set has two middle values: _____ and _____.

The median is the average of these two values:

$$\text{Median} = \frac{\boxed{} + \boxed{}}{2} = \boxed{}$$

REFLECT

2a. Why does the data set in **A** have one middle value while the data set in **B** has two middle values?

_____

_____

2b. The median is **sometimes** / **always** / **never** a value in the data set.

2c. Find the median of the data set in **1a**: 10, 9, 4, 8, 8, 3, 6, 8. How does the median compare to the mean?

_____

The mean and median of a data set may be equal, very close to each other, or very different from each other. For data sets where the mean and median differ greatly, one likely describes the data set better than the other.

3 EXPLORE   Mean or Median?

The monthly earnings of several teenagers are $200, $320, $275, $250, $750, $350, and $310.

A Find the mean.

$$\frac{\boxed{} + \boxed{} + \boxed{} + \boxed{} + \boxed{} + \boxed{} + \boxed{}}{\boxed{}} = \frac{\boxed{}}{\boxed{}} \approx \boxed{}$$

B Write the data values in order from least to greatest and find the median.

_____

C The mean and the median differ by about $_____. Why?

_____

_____

D Which measure of center better describes a typical teenager's monthly earnings—the mean or the median? Explain.

_____

_____

3a. Luka's final exam scores for this semester are 70, 72, 99, 72, and 69. Find the mean and median. Which is a better description of Luka's typical exam score?

_____

3b. Luka's parents ask Luka how his final exams went. Luka says, "My average exam score was about 76." Is Luka being truthful? Is Luka misleading his parents? Explain.

_____

_____

PRACTICE

Several students' scores on a history test are shown. Use these data for 1 and 2.

1. Mean ≈ _____   Median = _____

History Test Scores
73 45 88 90 90 81 83

2. Which measure better describes the typical score for these students? Explain.

_____

The points scored by a basketball team in its last 6 games are shown. Use these data for 3 and 4.

Points Scored
73 77 85 84 35 115

3. Mean ≈ _____   Median = _____

4. Which measure better describes the typical number of points scored? Explain.

_____

5. **Error Analysis** For two weeks, the school librarian recorded the number of library books returned each morning. The data are shown in the dot plot.

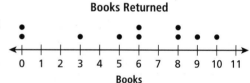

Books Returned

The librarian found the mean number of books returned each morning.

$$\frac{8 + 6 + 10 + 5 + 9 + 8 + 3 + 6}{8} = \frac{55}{8} = 6.9$$

Is this the correct mean of this data set? If not, explain and correct the error.

_____

_____

_____

_____

The *mode* of a data set is the data value that occurs most often. If all data values occur the same number of times, the data set is said to have no mode. Otherwise, a data set may have one or more modes. Find the mode(s) of each data set.

6. 5, 3, 7, 3, 9, 1, 7, 11   7. 34, 66, 22, 55, 23, 77   8. 400, 340, 870, 400

_____   _____   _____

Measures of Variability

COMMON CORE

CC.6.SP.2
CC.6.SP.3
CC.6.SP.4
CC.6.SP.5c, d

7-3

Essential question: *How can you use measures of variability to describe a data set?*

A **box plot** is a display that shows how the values in a data set are distributed, or spread out.

To make a box plot, first find five values for the data set:

- The least value
- The **lower quartile** — the median of the lower half of the data
- The median
- The **upper quartile** — the median of the upper half of the data
- The greatest value

1 EXAMPLE Box Plots

A **The heights of several students are shown. Make a box plot for the data.**

Students' Heights (in.)					
60	58	54	56	63	61
65	61	62	59	56	58

Step 1 Order the data and find the needed values.

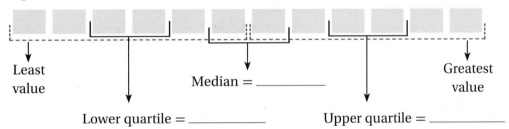

Least value

Lower quartile = _____

Median = _____

Upper quartile = _____

Greatest value

Step 2 Draw the box plot.

On the number line, draw dots above the least value, the lower quartile, the median, the upper quartile, and the greatest value.

Draw a rectangle (or box) above the number line. The left side of the box should pass through the dot for the lower quartile. The right side of the box should pass through the dot for the upper quartile.

Draw a vertical line segment from the top of the box, through the dot for the median, to the bottom of the box.

Draw horizontal line segments from the dot for the lower quartile to the dot for the least value and from the dot for the upper quartile to the dot for the greatest value.

Students' Heights

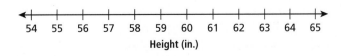

Height (in.)

B The heights of several different students are shown. Make a box plot of the data.

Students' Heights (in.)
46 47 48 48 56 48
46 52 57 52 45

Step 1 Order the data and find the needed values.

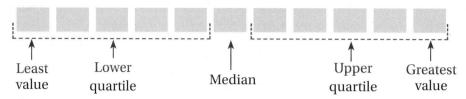

Least value Lower quartile Median Upper quartile Greatest value

Step 2 Draw the box plot.

Students' Heights

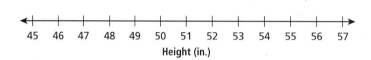

45   46   47   48   49   50   51   52   53   54   55   56   57

Height (in.)

REFLECT

1a. Compare the box plots in **A** and **B** . How do the box plots describe the distribution of the heights in each group?

_____

_____

_____

_____

A **measure of variability** is a single number that describes the spread of a data set. One measure of variability is the *interquartile range*. The **interquartile range (IQR)** is the difference of the upper quartile and the lower quartile.

2 **EXAMPLE** Finding the IQR

Find the IQR for the data sets in **1** .

A IQR = Upper quartile − Lower quartile

  = [ ] − [ ] = [ ]

B IQR = Upper quartile − Lower quartile

  = [ ] − [ ] = [ ]

REFLECT

2. Compare the IQRs. How do the IQRs describe the distribution of the heights in each group?

_____

_____

Another measure of variability is the *mean absolute deviation*. The **mean absolute deviation (MAD)** is the mean distance between each data value and the mean of the data set.

3 EXAMPLE Mean Absolute Deviation

Find the MAD for the data sets in ❶ **.**

Ⓐ 60, 58, 54, 56, 63, 61, 65, 61, 62, 59, 56, 58

Step 1 Find the mean. Round to the nearest whole number.

$$\frac{\boxed{} + \boxed{} + \boxed{} + \boxed{} + \boxed{} + \boxed{} + \boxed{} + \boxed{} + \boxed{} + \boxed{} + \boxed{} + \boxed{}}{\boxed{}} \approx \boxed{}$$

Step 2 Complete the table.

Height	60	58	54	56	63	61	65	61	62	59	56	58
Distance from Mean												

Step 3 To calculate the MAD, find the mean of the values in the second row of the table. Round to the nearest whole number.

$$\frac{\boxed{} + \boxed{} + \boxed{} + \boxed{} + \boxed{} + \boxed{} + \boxed{} + \boxed{} + \boxed{} + \boxed{} + \boxed{} + \boxed{}}{\boxed{}} \approx \boxed{}$$

Ⓑ 46, 47, 48, 48, 56, 48, 46, 52, 57, 52, 45

Step 1 Find the mean. Round to the nearest whole number.

$$\frac{\boxed{} + \boxed{} + \boxed{} + \boxed{} + \boxed{} + \boxed{} + \boxed{} + \boxed{} + \boxed{} + \boxed{} + \boxed{}}{\boxed{}} \approx \boxed{}$$

Step 2 Complete the table.

Height	46	47	48	48	56	48	46	52	57	52	45
Distance from Mean											

Step 3 To calculate the MAD, find the mean of the values in the second row of the table. Round to the nearest whole number.

$$\frac{\boxed{} + \boxed{} + \boxed{} + \boxed{} + \boxed{} + \boxed{} + \boxed{} + \boxed{} + \boxed{} + \boxed{} + \boxed{}}{\boxed{}} \approx \boxed{}$$

REFLECT

3. Compare the MADs. How do the MADs describe the distribution of the heights in each group?

_____

_____

The RBIs (Runs Batted In) for 15 players from the 2010 Seattle Mariners are shown. Use this data set for 1–6.

Mariners' RBIs
15 51 35 25 58 33 64
43 33 29 14 13 11 4 10

1. Find the median. _____

2. Find the lower quartile. _____

3. Find the upper quartile. _____

4. Make a box plot for the data.

Mariners' RBIs

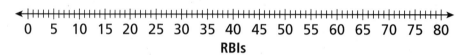

0   5   10   15   20   25   30   35   40   45   50   55   60   65   70   75   80

RBIs

5. Find the IQR. Round to the nearest whole number. _____

6. Find the MAD. Round to the nearest whole number. _____

The RBIs for 15 players from the 2010 Baltimore Orioles are shown. Use this data set for 7–12.

Orioles' RBIs
55 76 15 28 39 31 69
60 72 32 20 12 9 14 9

7. Find the median. _____

8. Find the lower quartile. _____

9. Find the upper quartile. _____

10. Make a box plot for the data.

Orioles' RBIs

0   5   10   15   20   25   30   35   40   45   50   55   60   65   70   75   80

RBIs

11. Find the IQR. Round to the nearest whole number. _____

12. Find the MAD. Round to the nearest whole number. _____

13. Using the information from 1–12, make a statement that compares the RBIs for the two teams.

_____

_____

UNIT 7

Problem Solving Connections

COMMON
CORE

CC.6.SP.1,
CC.6.SP.2,
CC.6.SP.3,
CC.6.SP.4,
CC.6.SP.5a, b,
c, d

You Big Chicken! Farmer Fred has been conducting an experiment with two pens of chickens. Since they were chicks, the chickens in pen A have been eating Premium Star chicken feed, while the chickens in pen B have been eating Rapid Growth chicken feed. Help Farmer Fred decide which feed produces larger chickens.

1 Display Numerical Data

A Farmer Fred will weigh the chickens in both pens at the end of his experiment. Is the question "How much do the chickens in each pen weigh?" a statistical question? Why or why not?

_____

B The weights that Farmer Fred records are shown in the tables.

Pen A – Premium Star Chickens' Weights (lb)				
6.4	5.2	7.5	8.3	5.6
7.6	8.1	7.7	6.2	6.4
8.1	4.8	5.5	6.6	6.7
4.9	5.1	8.1	7.9	7.5

Pen B – Rapid Growth Chickens' Weights (lb)				
6.6	5.1	7.7	8.1	5.7
5.7	4.5	7.4	6.1	6.3
7.9	4.9	5.6	6.4	6.8
4.7	5.3	6.0	8.0	6.6

How many chickens are in each pen? _____

What units are used to measure the chickens' weights? _____

C Make a dot plot of each data set.

Pen A – Premium Star

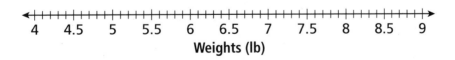

Weights (lb)

Pen B – Rapid Growth

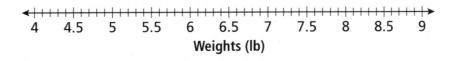

Weights (lb)

D Make a frequency table and histogram of the data for pen A.

Pen A – Premium Star	
Interval	Frequency
4.5–5.4	
5.5–6.4	
6.5–7.4	
7.5–8.4	

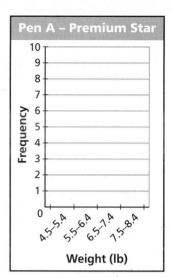

E Make a frequency table and histogram of the data for pen B.

Pen B – Rapid Growth	
Interval	Frequency
4.5–5.4	
5.5–6.4	
6.5–7.4	
7.5–8.4	

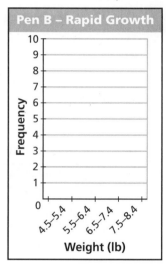

2 Measures of Center

A Find the mean and median weights of the chickens in pen A. Round to the nearest tenth if necessary.

B Find the mean and median weights of the chickens in pen B. Round to the nearest tenth if necessary.

3 Measures of Variability

A Find the lower quartile, upper quartile, least weight, and greatest weight of the chickens in pen A. Round to the nearest tenth if necessary.

B Make a box plot of the data for pen A.

Pen A – Premium Star

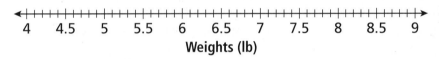

Weights (lb)

C Find the lower quartile, upper quartile, least weight, and greatest weight of the chickens in pen B. Round to the nearest tenth if necessary.

D Make a box plot of the data for pen B.

Pen B – Rapid Growth

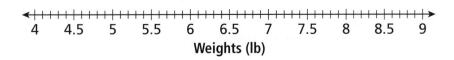

Weights (lb)

4 Answer the Question

A According to Farmer Fred's data, which feed produces larger chickens? Use information from the previous problems to support your answer.

_____

_____

_____

_____

B Which feed brand shows less variability among the weights of the chickens? How do you know? What does this mean?

_____

_____

_____

C Premium Star chicken feed costs $11.95 per bag. Rapid Growth chicken feed comes in a smaller bag that costs $10.25 per bag. Farmer Fred estimates that he would need 15 bags of Premium Star per month, or 20 bags of Rapid Growth per month.

Would Farmer Fred save money by using Rapid Growth instead of Premium Star? Explain.

D Do you think Farmer Fred would earn more money from his chickens by using Premium Star or Rapid Growth chicken feed? Explain.

_____

_____

_____

_____

E Based on all of the available information, I would recommend that Farmer Fred use Premium Star / Rapid Growth chicken feed.

Name _____ Class _____ Date _____

MULTIPLE CHOICE

Members of the school science club collected canned food for a food drive. The numbers of cans collected by 8 club members are shown. Use these data for 1–7.

Cans Collected							
4	10	5	11	15	7	3	9

1. What is the mean number of cans collected?

   A. 8   **C.** 10

   B. 9   **D.** 11

2. What is the median number of cans collected?

   F. 8   **H.** 10

   G. 9   **J.** 11

3. What is the upper quartile?

   A. 5   **C.** 10.5

   B. 7   **D.** 11

4. What is the lower quartile?

   F. 3   **H.** 5

   G. 4.5   **J.** 6

5. Which expression gives the interquartile range?

   A. $5 - 4$ **C.** $13.5 - 5$

   B. $10.5 - 4.5$ **D.** $15 - 3$

6. What is the mean average deviation?

   F. 3.25   **H.** 8

   G. 6.5   **J.** 26

7. What would be the leftmost and rightmost points on a box plot of these data?

   A. 3 and 15   **C.** 4.5 and 10.5

   B. 4 and 9   **D.** 6.5 and 8

Use the box plot for 8–13.

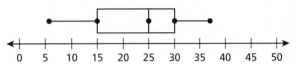

8. What is the median of this data set?

   F. 15   **H.** 30

   G. 25   **J.** 37

9. What is the least value of the data set?

   A. 5   **C.** 10

   B. 6   **D.** 11

10. What is the lower quartile?

    F. 15   **H.** 30

    G. 25   **J.** 40

11. Which is the best estimate of the difference of the greatest and least values?

    A. 10   **C.** 30

    B. 20   **D.** 40

12. Which expression gives the interquartile range?

    F. $30 - 15$

    G. $30 - 10$

    H. $30 - 5$

    J. $40 - 15$

13. Which question can be answered by reading the box plot?

    A. What is the mean?

    B. Which data value occurs most frequently?

    C. How many data values are there?

    D. The middle half of the data is between what two numbers?

14. Which of the following statements is **not** true?

   F. The median is a measure of the center of a data set.

   G. The mean is a measure of the variability of a data set.

   H. A dot plot shows the least and greatest values of a data set.

   J. A box plot shows the interquartile range.

FREE RESPONSE

The weights of Ann's chickens are shown. Use these data for 15–24.

Chickens' Weights (lb)											
14	6	5	7	7	5	6	7	6	6	4	5

15. How many chickens does Ann have?

_____

16. What unit in used to measure the chickens' weights?

_____

17. What is the mean weight of the chickens?

_____

18. What is the median weight of the chickens?

_____

19. Does the mean or the median better describe the center of this data set? Explain.

_____

_____

_____

20. Find the lower quartile and the upper quartile.

_____

_____

21. Find the interquartile range.

_____

22. a. Make a dot plot for the weights.

Ann's Chickens

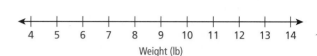

   b. Describe the shape of the data. Identify any gaps, clusters, or peaks. Are there any data values that do not fit the general shape? If so, which one(s)?

_____

_____

_____

23. Make a histogram for the weights.

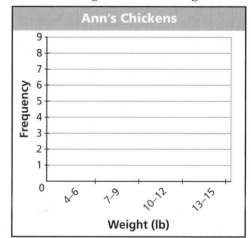

24. a. Make a box plot for the weights.

Ann's Chickens

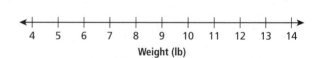

   b. How does the box plot describe the data set?

_____

_____

_____

Correlation of *On Core Mathematics Grade 6* to the Common Core State Standards

Ratios and Proportional Relationships	Citations
CC.6.RP.1 Understand the concept of a ratio and use ratio language to describe a ratio relationship between two quantities.	**pp. 113–116, 135–138**
CC.6.RP.2 Understand the concept of a unit rate *a/b* associated with a ratio *a:b* with *b* ≠ 0, and use rate language in the context of a ratio relationship.	**pp. 119–122, 135–138**
CC.6.RP.3 Use ratio and rate reasoning to solve real-world and mathematical problems, e.g., by reasoning about tables of equivalent ratios, tape diagrams, double number line diagrams, or equations. **a.** Make tables of equivalent ratios relating quantities with whole number measurements, find missing values in the tables, and plot the pairs of values on the coordinate plane. Use tables to compare ratios. **b.** Solve unit rate problems including those involving unit pricing and constant speed. **c.** Find a percent of a quantity as a rate per 100 (e.g., 30% of a quantity means 30/100 times the quantity); solve problems involving finding the whole, given a part and the percent. **d.** Use ratio reasoning to convert measurement units; manipulate and transform units appropriately when multiplying or dividing quantities.	**pp. 117–118, 119–122, 123–126, 127–130, 131–134, 135–138**

The Number System	Citations
CC.6.NS.1 Interpret and compute quotients of fractions, and solve word problems involving division of fractions by fractions, e.g., by using visual fraction models and equations to represent the problem.	**pp. 7–10, 29–32**
CC.6.NS.2 Fluently divide multi-digit numbers using the standard algorithm.	**pp. 3–6, 29–32**
CC.6.NS.3 Fluently add, subtract, multiply, and divide multi-digit decimals using the standard algorithm for each operation.	**pp. 11–14, 15–18, 19–22, 29–32**
CC.6.NS.4 Find the greatest common factor of two whole numbers less than or equal to 100 and the least common multiple of two whole numbers less than or equal to 12. Use the distributive property to express a sum of two whole numbers 1–100 with a common factor as a multiple of a sum of two whole numbers with no common factor.	**pp. 23–26, 27–28, 29–32**
CC.6.NS.5 Understand that positive and negative numbers are used together to describe quantities having opposite directions or values (e.g., temperature above/below zero, elevation above/below sea level, credits/debits, positive/negative electric charge); use positive and negative numbers to represent quantities in real-world contexts, explaining the meaning of 0 in each situation.	**pp. 37–38**

CC.6.NS.6 Understand a rational number as a point on the number line. Extend number line diagrams and coordinate axes familiar from previous grades to represent points on the line and in the plane with negative number coordinates. a. Recognize opposite signs of numbers as indicating locations on opposite sides of 0 on the number line; recognize that the opposite of the opposite of a number is the number itself, e.g., $-(-3) = 3$, and that 0 is its own opposite. b. Understand signs of numbers in ordered pairs as indicating locations in quadrants of the coordinate plane; recognize that when two ordered pairs differ only by signs, the locations of the points are related by reflections across one or both axes. c. Find and position integers and other rational numbers on a horizontal or vertical number line diagram; find and position pairs of integers and other rational numbers on a coordinate plane.	**pp. 37–38, 45–48, 51–54**
CC.6.NS.7 Understand ordering and absolute value of rational numbers. a. Interpret statements of inequality as statements about the relative position of two numbers on a number line diagram. b. Write, interpret, and explain statements of order for rational numbers in real-world contexts. c. Understand the absolute value of a rational number as its distance from 0 on the number line; interpret absolute value as magnitude for a positive or negative quantity in a real-world situation. d. Distinguish comparisons of absolute value from statements about order.	**pp. 39–42, 43–44, 51–54**
CC.6.NS.8 Solve real-world and mathematical problems by graphing points in all four quadrants of the coordinate plane. Include use of coordinates and absolute value to find distances between points with the same first coordinate or the same second coordinate.	**pp. 45–48, 49–50, 51–54**

Expressions and Equations	Citations
CC.6.EE.1 Write and evaluate numerical expressions involving whole-number exponents.	**pp. 59–62, 77–80**
CC.6.EE.2 Write, read, and evaluate expressions in which letters stand for numbers. a. Write expressions that record operations with numbers and with letters standing for numbers. b. Identify parts of an expression using mathematical terms (sum, term, product, factor, quotient, coefficient); view one or more parts of an expression as a single entity. c. Evaluate expressions at specific values of their variables. Include expressions that arise from formulas used in real-world problems. Perform arithmetic operations, including those involving whole-number exponents, in the conventional order when there are no parentheses to specify a particular order (Order of Operations).	**pp. 63–66, 67–68, 69–72, 77–80**
CC.6.EE.3 Apply the properties of operations to generate equivalent expressions.	**pp. 73–76, 77–80**
CC.6.EE.4 Identify when two expressions are equivalent (i.e., when the two expressions name the same number regardless of which value is substituted into them).	**pp. 73–76, 77–80**
CC.6.EE.5 Understand solving an equation or inequality as a process of answering a question: which values from a specified set, if any, make the equation or inequality true? Use substitution to determine whether a given number in a specified set makes an equation or inequality true.	**pp. 85–88, 101–104, 105–108**
CC.6.EE.6 Use variables to represent numbers and write expressions when solving a real-world or mathematical problem; understand that a variable can represent an unknown number, or, depending on the purpose at hand, any number in a specified set.	**pp. 63–66, 77–80, 85–88, 101–104, 105–108**
CC.6.EE.7 Solve real-world and mathematical problems by writing and solving equations of the form $x + p = q$ and $px = q$ for cases in which p, q and x are all nonnegative rational numbers.	**pp. 89–92, 93–96, 105–108**
CC.6.EE.8 Write an inequality of the form $x > c$ or $x < c$ to represent a constraint or condition in a real-world or mathematical problem. Recognize that inequalities of the form $x > c$ or $x < c$ have infinitely many solutions; represent solutions of such inequalities on number line diagrams.	**pp. 101–104, 105–108**
CC.6.EE.9 Use variables to represent two quantities in a real-world problem that change in relationship to one another; write an equation to express one quantity, thought of as the dependent variable, in terms of the other quantity, thought of as the independent variable. Analyze the relationship between the dependent and independent variables using graphs and tables, and relate these to the equation.	**pp. 97–100, 105–108**

Geometry	Citations
CC.6.G.1 Find the area of right triangles, other triangles, special quadrilaterals, and polygons by composing into rectangles or decomposing into triangles and other shapes; apply these techniques in the context of solving real-world and mathematical problems.	**pp. 143–146, 147–150, 151–154, 167–170**
CC.6.G.2 Find the volume of a right rectangular prism with fractional edge lengths by packing it with unit cubes of the appropriate unit fraction edge lengths, and show that the volume is the same as would be found by multiplying the edge lengths of the prism. Apply the formulas $V = l\,w\,h$ and $V = b\,h$ to find volumes of right rectangular prisms with fractional edge lengths in the context of solving real-world and mathematical problems.	**pp. 159–162, 167–170**
CC.6.G.3 Draw polygons in the coordinate plane given coordinates for the vertices; use coordinates to find the length of a side joining points with the same first coordinate or the same second coordinate. Apply these techniques in the context of solving real-world and mathematical problems.	**pp. 155–158**
CC.6.G.4 Represent three-dimensional figures using nets made up of rectangles and triangles, and use the nets to find the surface area of these figures. Apply these techniques in the context of solving real-world and mathematical problems.	**pp. 163–166**

Statistics and Probability	Citations
CC.6.SP.1 Recognize a statistical question as one that anticipates variability in the data related to the question and accounts for it in the answers.	**pp. 175–178, 187–190**
CC.6.SP.2 Understand that a set of data collected to answer a statistical question has a distribution which can be described by its center, spread, and overall shape.	**pp. 175–178, 179–182, 183–186, 187–190**
CC.6.SP.3 Recognize that a measure of center for a numerical data set summarizes all of its values with a single number, while a measure of variation describes how its values vary with a single number.	**pp. 179–182, 183–186, 187–190**
CC.6.SP.4 Display numerical data in plots on a number line, including dot plots, histograms, and box plots.	**pp. 175–178, 183–186, 187–190**
CC.6.SP.5 Summarize numerical data sets in relation to their context, such as by: a. Reporting the number of observations. b. Describing the nature of the attribute under investigation, including how it was measured and its units of measurement. c. Giving quantitative measures of center (median and/or mean) and variability (interquartile range and/or mean absolute deviation), as well as describing any overall pattern and any striking deviations from the overall pattern with reference to the context in which the data were gathered. d. Relating the choice of measures of center and variability to the shape of the data distribution and the context in which the data were gathered.	**pp. 175–178, 179–182, 183–186, 187–190**